Fort King George

—

Step One to Statehood

Replica of John Barnwell's 1721 Fort King George, Darien,
Georgia, with Historic Site personnel in period costume
(Photograph courtesy of Rundle Cook)

Fort King George

—

Step One to Statehood

JEANNINE COOK

Book Design : Venessa Rand, Design Press, Savannah
Printed by The Darien News, Darien

The paper in this book meets the guidelines for permanence
and durability of the Committee on Production Guidelines for Book
Longevity of the Council on Library Resources.

Printed in the United States of America

Library of Congress Catalogue Card Number : 90-91655

COVER:
Replica of John Barnwell's 1721 Fort King George,
Darien, Georgia
(Photograph courtesy of Georgia Department of Natural Resources)

BACK COVER:
1721 British Jack

For Rundle

CONTENTS

ILLUSTRATIONS

ACKNOWLEDGEMENTS

In my preparation of this short history, I am greatly indebted to the late Miss Bessie Lewis of McIntosh County, Georgia. Her pioneering research and historical insights enabled me to use contemporary documents largely to tell their own story of Fort King George.

Mr. Ken Akins, Superintendent, Mr. Bill Merriman and Mrs. Doris Rabb of the Georgia Department of Natural Resources' Fort King George Historic Site all afforded me appreciated assistance, with Ken Akins being my guide to recent history.

Mr. Malcolm Bell, Jr. of Savannah, Georgia, gave me encouragement and help in a generous and timely fashion. I am most grateful to him.

Finally, it is with warmest appreciation that I acknowledge the assistance of the Mills B. Lane Foundation in enabling me to publish this document and have it distributed under the aegis of Darien's Lower Altamaha Historical Society.

INTRODUCTION

The first fort built at the mouth of the Altamaha River was constructed in 1721. The present Fort King George has had a slow but rewarding resurrection. Its renewed existence lends distinction to Darien, McIntosh County, in coastal Georgia.

Little mention of the original Fort King George is found in historical records between 1736 and the early 1900s. It was in 1736, under the auspices of General Oglethorpe, that 177 Scottish Highlanders founded the town of Darien on the bluffs above the Altamaha River. Although the Fort site was called Barnwell's Bluff (after the Fort's builder, Colonel John Barnwell), Old Fort King George Bluff or Lower Bluff, the Fort itself, or what little remained of its timber buildings and earthworks, slept under a heavy cloak of vegetation flourishing in Georgia's sub-tropical climate. History was repeating itself. Early Woodland Period Indians had already lived in the area three thousand years before. Later the Spanish had interacted briefly with Coastal Indians in the sixteenth century. However, vegetation and erosion had camouflaged most of their traces before the British arrived in 1721.

Evidently the Fort still existed physically to some degree in 1772 for the "Old Fort" on the "North Branch of Altamaha River" is shown by a fort symbol on Philip Young's survey of 3rd August, 1772. (1) Soon after, botanist William Bartram visited Darien and wrote, "about

a mile below the Town on a Bluff of the River, remains part
of one of the Angles of the Fort [,] the River having so far
incroached on the Bluff caried it with the foundation of the
Fort to the Point of an Island opposite which increases
constantly & the deepest part of this entrance of the River,
runs where the Fort stood." (2)

By 1803, a two-storey tabby house 20 ft. x 40 ft. (the
foundations of which still stand) was being built on "the
old fort bluff [so called] one mile below Darien" for
Hamden McIntosh, according to Reuben King's Journal. (3)

Soon after, some time between 1806 and 1822,
sawmilling operations brought new life to the high bluffs
along the Altamaha River. Prime virgin timber was rafted
down the Altamaha from inland forests to Darien. There, at
the Lower Bluff site, a tidal-powered mill first operated,
followed by a steam-powered sawmill. About 1817, several
planters and businessmen joined Mr. Jacob Rockenbaugh
to form the Darien Eastern Saw Mill Company. By 1824,
their sawmill building, 120 ft. long by 64 ft. wide, housed a
larger steam engine and by 1831, five gangs of saws were
operating there. The log channels were adapted from the
Fort's earthworks, earth fortifications were levelled and
timber debris and ballast from incoming lumber ships
were used as fill in an area east of the old Fort site along
the River.

Sawmilling continued until Georgia's forests were
depleted after the turn of this century. Ownership of the
Darien Lower Bluff mill had passed to the Hilton Timber &
Lumber Company by 1878, and the Hilton family operated
the large steam-driven mill until 1906 when heavy timber
became scarce. Smaller logs were processed by a circular
sawmill which operated from about 1905 to 1914.

Silence fell once more on Barnwell's Bluff when the
lumber era came to an end. In November, 1926, Sea Island
Investments Incorporated purchased the 12-acre site from
the Savannah River Lumber Company. Meanwhile, a

young lady from Ohio, Miss Bessie Lewis, had arrived in McIntosh County. Her deep interest in history led, in time, to the rediscovery of Fort King George.

By comparing maps of the Lower Bluff area from Colonial Records with modern maps, Miss Lewis was able to pinpoint the possible site of Fort King George at the river's curve. Her exhaustive research of historical records, together with Mr. R. D. Fox's location of the old mill sites in 1939, laid the foundation for the Georgia State Department of Natural Resources to acquire the Lower Bluff Tract on 29th June, 1940, "for the purpose of securing a State Park and to improve the same as a State Park and as the Site of Old Fort King George ..." (4)

The Fort King George State Park was initially administered by the Parks Division. Archaeological excavations in a fifty foot square were carried out in 1940 by Joseph R. Caldwell during a survey of the Georgia Coast. He uncovered remains of an Indian structure and 15 graves, presumably of British soldiers who died at the Fort. Excavations were resumed in 1950 to complete the investigation of the Indian house. In March, 1952, the Georgia Historical Commission hired Sheila Caldwell, an archaeologist with the University of Georgia, to pursue excavations at the Fort Site. A Spanish Mission building and several Indian structures were exciting discoveries, but the presence of 65 more shallow graves, with bodies buried in Christian fashion, appeared to confirm the site as being that of Fort King George, graveyard of many a British soldier.

The Historic Site was deeded to the Georgia Historical Commission in 1961 and began to attract more interest. Markers were placed on the soldiers' graves by the Daughters of the American Revolution. A campaign, spearheaded by Dr. William Tailer, President of the Darien-McIntosh County Chamber of Commerce, was launched in 1965 to raise funds to restore Fort King George and to persuade Georgia's Governor Carl Sanders to allocate monies to develop the Fort, possibly "one of Georgia's finest assets" according to Mrs. Mary Gregory Jewett, Executive Secretary of the Georgia Historical Commission. (5)

By December, 1965, Darien was given the choice by the Georgia Historical Commission of either spending acquired funds on a reconstructed fort or on a museum (thus furthering historical education) and a Superintendent's residence (to secure the Site). The Fort's reconstruction was postponed.

In 1967, archaeological excavations were carried out on the proposed sites of the museum and residence by Marian Brasington, under guidance of Lewis H. Larson, Jr., professor of anthropology at Georgia State College. Archaeologist William M. Kelso also surveyed the proposed Superintendent's residence site in 1967, concluding in his 1968 report that the sawmill and Spanish Mission eras should mostly be emphasised at the Historic Site.

The Museum was dedicated in 1970 and the first Superintendent of Fort King George, Bruce King, took up residence. In 1975, the Site came under the jurisdiction of the Georgia Department of Natural Resources, Parks and Historic Sites Division. Work continued on clearing the Site and enhancing the Museum during the next decade. By 1981, when a visitation fee was imposed, the Fort Site's image was however at its nadir in tourists' eyes. Despite large signs on the highways leading to Darien announcing "FORT King George Historic Site", visitors found there was no fort to be seen and turned around to leave in disgust.

The reconstruction of the Fort had always been a dream for Miss Bessie Lewis and others, such as Dr. Tailer and, later, William G. Haynes, Jr. They and other citizens had expended immense efforts over the years in lobbying legislators and government officials alike to allocate funds for this reconstruction. Finally these efforts paid off when the then president of the local Lower Altamaha Historical Society, William B. Dean, asked a British-born newcomer to McIntosh County, Rundle Cook, to take steps to achieve this goal.

At Rundle Cook's suggestion, Mr. Dean agreed to write to Georgia Department of Natural Resources Commissioner J. Leonard Ledbetter, committing the Lower Altamaha Historical Society to provide the State with the proceeds of a $50,000 fund drive on a gentleman's understanding that the State would construct a true replica of John Barnwell's 1721 blockhouse fort with these monies. The State agreed.

The extensive fund-raising campaign achieved and finally surpassed the $50,000 goal … thanks to such major donors as the Mills B. Lane Foundation, the McIntosh County Commissioners and the City of Darien, as well as innumerable private and corporate contributors. Meanwhile, Senator Glenn Bryant, then serving on the State Parks Appropriations Committee, helped secure a further $60,000 from State funds which ensured the construction in 1987 of an Audio-Visual Room and maintenance shed and helped to pay for the blockhouse frame.

Reconstruction of the blockhouse fort, 26 ft. square in oak post and beam frame, began in May, 1988, after exhaustive research into all aspects of its construction. Edward Ware Rowley, a McIntosh County native and architect, combined Barnwell's building records with data generously supplied by Parks Canada, the National Parks Services at Saratoga, New York, Mr. J. W. Baker (who researched 16th century post and beam construction in England for Plymouth Foundation) and Mr. Roy Underhill, master craftsman at Colonial Williamsburg and author of "Wood Wright's Workshop" on Public Television. Mr. Rowley also worked with engineer Dole Kelley, designer of the world's largest wooden structure, to ensure the safety of the blockhouse foundations on the unstable landfill site dating from the sawmill era. The D.N.R. staff, under O.R. Cothran III, played their part in ensuring the best possible use of the donated funds.

The faithfully reconstructed Fort and surrounding earthworks were formally declared open on 23rd October, 1988, by Lieutenant Colonel David H.A. Shephard, Queens, British Liaison Officer at Fort Benning, Georgia, who represented the British Ambassador to the United States of America. The British soldiers' graves, decorated with Union Jacks, were blessed during a short ceremony by the Very Reverend Dean Hay and the Reverend Stephen B. Barnwell, direct descendant of Colonel John Barnwell. A colour guard and regimental band from Fort Stewart led the large crowd of honoured guests and visitors to the Fort towering high above the Georgia marshes.

Today, a 1721 British flag floats proudly by the cypress-clad Fort. Furnishings and cannon still need to be added to complete the Fort; plans of reconstructed barracks and dock are now evoked ... Residents of McIntosh County are increasingly appreciating "their" Fort King George. Revenues and visitor attendance have more than doubled in the time since the Fort's reconstruction.

As hard-working Ken Akins, Superintendent of Fort King George Historic Site, has discovered, local people now enquire, regularly and enthusiastically, "What's going on at the Fort?" John Barnwell would have been vastly gratified to hear that said when he embarked on his fort-building project on the Altamaha River bluff 269 years ago.

A crane lifts a 'bent', a section of the oak posts and beams,
into place as Fort King George rises again in 1988
(Photograph courtesy of Rundle Cook)

**Fort King George's
reconstruction - roof
rafters are set in place**
(Photograph courtesy
of Rundle Cook)

**An upward view of the oak frame
of the reconstructed Fort**
(Photograph courtesy of the
Georgia Department of Natural Resources)

Fort King George

—

Step One to Statehood

Chapter One

Background History

The early 1700s saw the energetic colonists in South Carolina in a continuous state of apprehension about the safety of their borders. Although the north and south limits of the Carolinas were defined by Charles II's Royal Charter in 1663 as 36° 30′ and 29° respectively, these were abstract concepts to the Carolinians for they relied more on actual possession of territory. They regarded the Savannah River as delimiting the area beyond which hostile Indians, French and Spanish represented an ever-present threat to Charles Town, Port Royal and the increasing numbers of prosperous rice, cattle and indigo plantations.

South Carolina had a white population of 6, 250 by 1715, with 10, 500 blacks. Not only were there powerful planters along the coast, but yeoman farmers cultivating corn and cattle on the colony's frontiers. Beyond travelled the South Carolinian intrepids, the Indian traders, ranging far into the interior.

These traders extended South Carolinian and hence British influence westward to the Mississippi River among the many Indian tribes. Their trade was based upon deerskins, exported in vast numbers to England from Charles Town, and Indian slaves, sold locally, in New England and even to the West Indies. In return traders purveyed woollens and haberdashery, hardware and tools, arms and ammunition, tobacco and rum … to the Indians, using their trade to ensure allegiance to Charles Town whenever possible.

The dawn of the eighteenth century heralded an intensified struggle for control of the Southeastern portion of North America between France, Spain and England. The Carolinians had long been recognised as the most aggressive and skilful in wooing the Indians. However, the tribes' shifting loyalties to the different white contenders for land and trade resulted in a constantly changing situation in those wilderness politics. Indeed, the Spanish and French, although often handicapped by scanty finances and sparse supplies of trade goods, fought back energetically to win over the Indians and push back implicit British territorial challenges. In 1717, the Spanish had ensured the allegiance of the Apalache and Creek Indians by sending a delegation of seven of their chiefs to the Viceroy in Mexico. By that same year, the English were again wresting influence from the French traders as far inland as Bienville's Fort Toulouse. It had been built as a British "fur factory" trading site on the Alabama river which the French had taken over in 1715.

The French, based in America's interior from the Mississippi to the Great Lakes and Canada, were also eyeing the Altamaha River's potential as an artery for their traders and priests to the Atlantic. Their territorial aspirations, fired in part by Louis XIV's ambitions to extend France's dominion, were even reflected in contemporary maps published in Europe. Guillaume Delisle, Royal Geographer to the King of France, published one map in 1718 entitled "A New Map of the North Parts of America claimed by France". On it, the French claimed as theirs land from the Mississippi to the coast at Edisto River in South Carolina, along the coast to the Savannah River and the "Margravate of Azilia", Sir Robert

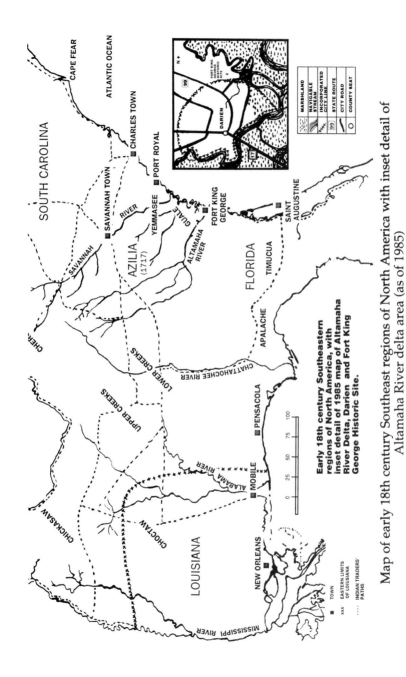

Map of early 18th century Southeast regions of North America with inset detail of
Altamaha River delta area (as of 1985)

**Early 18th century Southeastern
regions of North America, with
inset detail of 1985 map of Altamaha
River Delta, Darien and Fort King
George Historic Site.**

3

Montgomery's tract of land between the Savannah and Altamaha Rivers to which he received title in 1717. Since he did not settle his planned fortified town (covering 20 square miles), the grant became void after three years. Nonetheless, the French were hoping to push their sphere of influence right to the Southeast coast of North America.

The Spanish string of mission settlements along Guale, the Southeastern Atlantic coastal region, had progressively failed because of Indian depredations, resulting from English manipulation of the Indian tribes. However, the Spanish, from their secure base at St. Augustine in Florida, still had aspirations of revitalising former settlements. They therefore regarded British claims to land north of Florida as spurious and were, in any case, in a de facto alliance with the French against the English in North America.

The South Carolinians' often uneasy co-existence with their Indian neighbours had meanwhile degenerated into the savage Yemassee War in 1715; this led to these Indians mainly retreating north of the Savannah River or southwards to the Spanish in Florida after they were defeated. Alliances with other tribes nearby were in a constant state of flux, requiring continual attention from Indian Commissioners and the Provincial Government.

The Carolinians' concerns about possible French and Spanish encroachments were first voiced to the Lords Proprietors of South Carolina in England. England at that time was controlled by the Whig party ministers, Stanhope and Townsend. They effectively ruled the country for George I, a German who spoke no English and interested himself little in his new kingdom's affairs. The Lords Proprietors responsible for the colony were never very attentive to South Carolina's needs. So when the Lords Commissioners for Trade and Plantations were established in 1696, the Board of Trade, as it was commonly known, became the object of petitions and appeals from disgruntled Carolinians. By 1719, South Carolina was bitterly reproaching the Lords Proprietors for their reactionary rule, lack of support during the desperate 1715 Indian War and their failure to protect the beleaguered colony from increasing French encirclement. Finally the colony rebelled, overthrew the government and elected its own Governor. South Carolina thus passed under direct Royal rule (although the Lords Proprietors did not relinquish final control until 1729) and Francis Nicholson was appointed Provisional Governor of the Colony.

By that time, there was such ferment about the need to secure South Carolina's southern borders that a deputation of the colony's two most persuasive men was sent to London in March, 1720, to present the Board of Trade with a plan of action. Joseph Boone was the English agent for South Carolina. John Barnwell was a highly respected, competent and energetic Irishman who had settled in South Carolina in 1701, "passed thro' all the public offices except that of Governor" (1) and become a very successful planter in the Port Royal area. He had grown to know the Carolinas well. In 1711, he had helped rescue fellow colonists in North Carolina when they were threatened by Tuscarora Indians (thereby earning the sobriquet 'Tuscarora Jack').

Later, in 1716, he had gone far south of the Savannah River to dislodge the Huspaw Indians from their home along the Altamaha River and force them southwards to Florida. He is also thought to have made a map by 1720 of the Carolinas and present-day Georgia, for a large, unsigned and undated map is attributed to him. (2) The Journal for July 28th, 1720, of the Commissioners for Trade and Plantations states "… That most of the maps yet extant of these parts are erroneous, as Colonel Barnwell, who is reputed to be, among the English, the best acquainted with that country, reports, and who is now preparing a new map of it". (3)

His detailed knowledge of the land between the Savannah and Altamaha Rivers was much sought after in London. When he arrived in March, 1720, the English were in the throes of feverish land speculation, known as the South Sea Bubble. One of the speculator-dreamers had been Sir Robert Montgomery with his 1717 proposal to settle the Margravate of Azilia north of the Altamaha River. Barnwell wrote to Montgomery to elaborate on the beauty of the region; his letter was published in pamphlet form in "A Description of the Golden Islands". Barnwell's support for Montgomery's scheme diminished as his own projects prospered, however, and by September, he was actively campaigning against Azilia as being a threat to his proposals to the Board of Trade. Meanwhile, during those speculative times, eager private investors sought Barnwell out daily at the Birchin Lane Carolina Coffee House, which he frequented, or at the home of Francis Nicholson, South Carolina's next Governor. His advice was also sought by members of the Board of Trade, the Privy Council and even Lord Townsend, President of the Privy Council.

On this visit to London, Boone and Barnwell presented the Board of Trade with the concept of a series of strategically-placed frontier forts to contain French expansion in the Southeastern region, with accompanying settlements. Barnwell suggested Port Royal should become a port of entry and the supply centre for the whole southern frontier. Implicit in the proposal was the expansion of British influence to the South and West. Not only would the six proposed forts act as a deterrent to Britain's rivals in the area and eliminate the expense of the existent scout boats protecting South Carolina's southern coastline and border, but the settlements would ensure trade continued with Indians to the West, thereby curtailing French influence.

Indeed, Barnwell and Boone reminded the Board that "the Method of the French is to build Forts on their

Frontiers which it would be to our Interest to do likewise, not only to preserve Our Trade with the Indians and their Dependence upon Us, but to preserve our Boundaries". (4) Fears that "the French particularly pretend a Right to the River May (Altamaha)" harked back to the ever-present concerns about any loss of control of territory imperilling trade with the Indians.

As Richard Berresford, agent to London for the South Carolina Assembly, had written to the Board of Trade in December, 1717, about the possibility of the French destroying the British-Cherokee alliance, "We shall not only lose all our Commerce with the Natives which will Sink our Trade but be evidently expos'd to be drove out of the Continent by the French and their Numerous Allies; and what a Loss as well as Disgrace this will be to England 'tis not easy to be conceiv'd and far less to be express'd." (5)

Arthur Middleton, President and Commander in Chief of South Carolina, later put it even more bluntly. In September, 1725, he wrote to the Duke of Newcastle, Principal Secretary of State, about the danger of the Spanish taking possession of the Altamaha River, saying "they will entirely deprive this province of all the trade and obedience of the Western Indians, which will not only leave us naked & defenseless, but greatly hinder the consumption of the woollens and other British manufactures". (6)

Chapter Two

The Altamaha River Garrison

The Board of Trade members agreed with the South Carolinian plan of a screen of forts on the southern border and forwarded Barnwell's and Boone's plan to the Lords Justices. Conservative and realist, they were less imperialistic than the Board of Trade. Accordingly they recommended to the Privy Council that only the Altamaha garrison be funded, with Barnwell to oversee the project. These recommendations specified that the garrison was to be situated "at or near the mouth of the River Alatamaha in South Carolina".

Other considerations were evoked: it would also be "very convenient for his Majesty's service that a certain Extent of Ground adjoining to the place where the new Fort shall be erected should be marked out, and set apart in equal lots not exceeding half an acre in such lot nor 100 acres in the whole to build a town upon in time to come in case this settlement should prosper, as 'tis hoped it will. And further that a reservation should likewise be made of 600 acres circumjacent to the said prospected town for common Pasturage for the Inhabitants of the sd. town when built." (1) Further encouragement to settle the area would be in the form of grants up to 200 acres of land to any inhabitant of the town.

Evidently John Barnwell impressed everyone in London with whom he had dealings, for the same letter to the Lords Justices goes on to say, "Among the papers referred to us; there is one Entituled an Account of necessaries for 100 men now bound to South Carolina which we have perused, ... recommended by Coll. Barnwell who seems to be a very intelligent person in these matters, so far as the said necessaries do relate to the Sd' new Settlement only, ... we conceive it may be for his Majesty's Service that the same should be forthwith provided."

Arrangements included a proposal for the Governor to be empowered to hire a Sloop or Brigantine to guard the men while the fort was being built. Since Governor Nicholson was to be on the spot, it was also proposed that he have full powers to carry out the planned construction and garrisoning of the fort. The Governor also requested that an "able Engineer" be sent on the expedition, together with a "proportionable number of Gunners and Maltrosses". It was finally suggested that "Genl. Nicholson should be directed after the new intended Fort should be built to put the same together with ye Garrison under the care and Government of the said Col. Barnwell whose knowledge of the Country and experience in matters of this Nature will highly conduce to the promoting of a settlement on this Frontier". (2)

The Privy Council reviewed all these recommendations and approved the construction of the fort on the Altamaha River, considered the most vital point for South Carolina's protection and the curtailment of French expansion to the East. Governor Nicholson was sent the requisite instructions for this project. (3)

The English had already had considerable experience with fort building, both in Europe and in the American colonies. In 1622, the Plymouth Pilgrims had a blockhouse at their fort, described by Issack de Rasières, Secretary of New Netherlands: "Upon the hill they have a large square

Blockhouse silhouette showing loopholes, portholes
and overhang for machicolation
(Photograph courtesy of Georgia Department of Natural Resources)

Fort King George under construction,
showing the outer palisading
(Photograph courtesy of Georgia Department of Natural Resources)

house, with a flat roof, built of thick sawn planks stayed with oak beams, upon the top of which they have 6 canon, which shoot iron balls of 4 and 5 pounds, and command the surrounding country..." (4)

The word 'Blockhouse' probably stems from 'Blochaus', a German word meaning 'a house which blocks a pass'. Blockhouses probably developed in Northern America, particularly in New England, as a response to wilderness conditions and defensive problems. As Barnwell may have emphasised to the Board of Trade, constructing a garrison fort with a small blockhouse involved modest expenditures of time, money and labour. A blockhouse was simple and strong, easy to construct and readily adaptable to local building materials. Indeed, single-family blockhouses were frequently built during the 17th century throughout the colonies to provide protection for a family

Re-enacted defences at the reconstructed Fort
(Photograph courtesy of Rundle Cook)

Present-day living history re-enactments at Fort King George
showing the use of ordnance portholes and machicolation
(Photograph courtesy of Georgia Department of Natural Resources)

and for neighbours in times of crisis. There was, for instance, a traders' blockhouse which had from early days overlooked the focus of western trading trails at Savannah Town on the north banks of the Savannah River at the fall line.

The standard form of blockhouse in North America with which Barnwell would have been familiar was a "single structure, two storeys high with an overhanging second storey, loopholes and portholes for ordnance, and machicolation in the overhang". (5)

The first basic defence of any blockhouse was the palisading around it, with ditches beyond this picketing. Blockhouse walls were of timber, and overhangs and machicolations gave the blockhouse its distinctive form. Holes cut in the floor of an overhanging upper storey allowed defenders to fire downwards (machicoulis) on an enemy who had breached the palisades and reached the blockhouse.

Details of joints in Fort King George's post and beam oak frame

1. Dovetailing and a mortise, together with pegholes

2. A tenon protruding, ready to fit a mortise, and peg holes

3. Peg holes and bevelled halving

4. Peg ready to be driven to secure the joint

(Photographs courtesy of Rundle Cook)

This second storey, higher than the palisades, was a place of final retreat from which defenders could direct a formidable barrage of fire power in all directions, through loopholes cut in the walls and ordnance portholes cut in the upper storey walls. Roofs were steep-pitched against snow in the north but against heavy rains in Barnwell's planned blockhouse.

Blockhouses were frequently erected to guard narrow river channels, portages, harbours and canals. Small garrisons at these points were intended to harass an enemy if he appeared and delay him; the blockhouses could also be quickly evacuated if the need arose. They helped maintain and protect extended lines of communication and provide local defences, with a minimum expenditure of money. "Most blockhouses were temporary answers to the basic dilemma of money and security." (6)

According to research done by Richard Harris in March, 1986, for a proposed new fort at Plimouth Plantation, Mass., 17th century blockhouses were a very sturdy assembly of wooden posts and beams, their mortises and tenons and other joints pegged firmly together. Floor beams were 12" x 12", as were the braced posts, while floor joists, wall plates, purlins or rafters were proportionately massive. Studs were a minimum of 7" x 3", while the vertical boards were sturdy enough to withstand arrows or musket fire. Gunports were left open to allow 360 degrees vision. Ground floors were of rammed earth, while upper floors were of 1" boards. The observation platform was left open to the elements. Stairs were made of solid triangular treads, in straight flights and not very steeply pitched.

Preparations for the new fort on the Altamaha River were methodical. Barnwell, well aware of the tasks ahead in construction of such a blockhouse-fort in the heat of summer, in hostile territory, was already writing to the President of the Council on November 8th, 1720, saying, "Difficulties expected, therefore men chosen ... to secure the possession of St. George on Alatamaha River ... should be young robust men able to undergo fatigue, and if possible such men as have been abroad on former expeditions." (7) He also urged allocation of tracts of land to these soldiers as further inducement to them to serve at this fort.

The 100 men to be sent to the new fort were officially raised as an Independent Company of Foot, commissioned at Whitehall on September 24th, 1720. However, instead of being vigorous young soldiers, the men sent to South Carolina were invalids and older veterans of European campaigns fought during the War of the Spanish Succession, men recruited from standing Invalid Companies. Hardly the pioneering stock to open up a new area and defend it.

The men had been directed to report to the Governors of Plymouth or Portsmouth; they carried their firelock, bayonet, sword and other equipment. Instructions to the Governor at Plymouth emphasised that secrecy was required about sending the company "of the ablest and best men" overseas "to prevent a desertion which may otherwise be apprehended". (8) Serving King and Country in the colonies in those times really implied being exiled for life.

The Captain of the Independent Company of Foot was to be General Francis Nicholson, also the Provisional Governor of South Carolina. His experience of North American colonies was already very wide, for he had served as Governor in Maryland and later in Virginia. He had also been Lieutenant Governor of New York and thus Captain of one of the two New York Independent Companies. Nicholson had long been aware of the threat to the British from French expansionist movements from Canada to the Gulf of Mexico and their friendship with Indian tribes. He had always sought to check French activities by fostering British trade westward from the seaboard colonies, especially from New York and South Carolina. Nicholson's appointment to South Carolina was thus no accident. Even the Board of Trade concurred with him by 1720 that South Carolina, with its extensive trade with the Indians west to the Mississippi and beyond and its experience in border conflicts with Spanish Florida, was the logical headquarters of English opposition to the French in the American Southeast.

The Independent Company's officers also came from the Invalid Companies. Lieutenant Joseph Lambert came from Colonel Fielding's Regiment garrisoned at Portsmouth, as did Ensign Thomas Merryman. Lieutenant John Emmenes came from Colonel Symond's Company at Plymouth and Ensign John Bowdler from one of the ten new Independent Companies of Invalids stationed in Jersey. Robert Mason was also commissioned Surgeon and Thomas Hesketh as Chaplain after service in the West Indies from 1696, followed by the Marines and 32nd Foot. These men's commissions were issued by the Lords Justices instead of the King, for he probably was still uninterested in his American Colonies.

Orders were issued for six months' advance subsistence, ordnance stores and equipment to be supplied and loaded aboard the two chartered vessels, the MARY and the CAROLINA GALLEY. There were the inevitable delays. Troops and stores waited in port until 8th March, 1721, for the warship detailed to escort the convoy to America. General Nicholson checked the ordnance and exchanged some for better weapons. He also had Mr. Richard Arnold of the War Office appointed agent on 13th September, 1720, to ensure regular payment of his Company and prompt settlement of accounts.

Chapter Three

Preparations in Charles Town

The convoy of the two troopships and HMS ENTERPRISE did not reach South Carolina until May, 1721. By this time, the 41st Independent Company was in very poor condition. On May 20th, 1721, Joseph Lambert, John Emmenes, Thomas Merryman, John Bowdler and Robert Mason wrote to the South Carolina Council and Governor in these terms: "We the Commissioned officers and surgeon belonging to Your Excellency's Independent Company of Foot aboard the Mary and Carolina Galley do certify that ye soldiers aboard are dangerously ill of the Scurvy and we are very short of all manner of Provisions so that we humbly beg that Your Excellency would be pleased to order them to be landed at Charles Town that they may have fresh provisions which is the only means of their recovery." (1)

Evidently everyone aboard was much exercised about being obliged to continue directly to Port Royal and then to the Altamaha River as had been ordered. On May 23rd, 1721, Captains Daniel Bell and John Smyte wrote to Governor Nicholson, "After a long passage hear we bless God we are safe arrived at the Barr of Charles Town. Our Water is short and Provisions almost gone, and our Soldiers half down with the Scurvey, and in case we should go for Port Royal we may be a month at this time of the year before we get there. Before that time our men may be half dead, as also there is no Pilot to be had for Port Royal, we therefore beg the favour of your Excellency that we may go in here and not endanger the soldiers' lives."(2)

On behalf of the Ship's Company under his command, J. Yeo wrote to the Governor on May 24th in the same vein - sickness after such a tedious passage amongst soldiers and sailors combined with the prospect of a slow passage to Port Royal would probably prove "fatal"... (3) He thus requested that the Governor allow them to land at Charles Town.

On September 10th, 1720, Colonel John Barnwell had written out his "Account of necessarys to be provided for ye use of ye 100 men now bound to South Carolina" and also offered to supervise their supply, saying, "I putt these things down that you might know whether they are sufficient stores and if there is occasion I am ready to wait on those that shall be appointed to procure the things and advise them in the choice of them". (4) His list ranges from "a skillfull Surgeon with a chest of medicines, a gunsmith with his forge, a cooper with 6 setts of coopers tools" to "2 doz.n iron potts of different sizes, 1000 fishing hooks of different sizes, 1000 ells Ozenbriggs for sumr. clothing" or "200 pair of stockins". 'Tuscarora Jack' had tried to think of everything that a small group of men might require on such a venture into the wilds where the nearest supplies were at least 6 days away by boat. Saws, hachets, spades, pickaxes and shovels, grind stones and hand mills, wedges, corkage for boats, deep sea lines or graplins were all required.

The ENTERPRISE convoy brought to Charles Town not only the 100 soldiers recruited to garrison the Fort, but also Barnwell and Governor Nicholson. The energetic pioneer and the older soldier-administrator had worked closely together in dealings with the Board of Trade and other officials in London, but they must have got to know each

other well during the tedious Atlantic crossing. They
certainly discussed the Fort project, its strategic
implications and difficulties attendant upon its execution,
especially in view of the soldiers' condition. Later
exchanges of documents between the two men bespeak of
a respect for each other, each united further by their desire
to serve King and Country.

Neither lost any time after their arrival in Charles Town.
The Governor was officially welcomed on May 29th. On
3rd June, 1721, Barnwell laid a memorandum before the
Governor and his Council as had been requested the
previous day by Order of Council. In it, he outlined "by
what methods I propose to carry in and effect the building
of a Fort on the Alatamaha River, and what Instruction I
shall think may be necessary for that purpose". He
reminded Nicholson that "when the Regency thought it
necessary for his Majesty's service to have the said
settlement made, they gave their orders to the Board of
Ordinance on the 12th of October last to provide an
Engineer, artificers with tools sufficient to enable ye
Excellency to do the same effectually".

He went on, "Yr Excellency may also remember that
upon application made to the Board of Ordinance they
raised many difficulties in relation to the artificers, though
they furnished the tools and an engineer, who, though he
received six months pay had likewise disappointed Yr
Excellency". He addressed the problem of the invalid
soldiers : "Though it was represented by Brigadier General
Richards and Coll. Bogard of the Board of Ordinance, that
the readiest way to procure Trades Men was to have them
broughted out of the standing Regiments, together with
your able men fit to undergo labour and hardships. Yet
notwithstanding the utmost application made by Yr.
Excellency you were ordered one hundred invalids, who
are for the most part unable to perform any labour, and
whom the least hardships will destroy, and more especially

this unreasonable time of the year. Now under these circumstances vizt. without an Engineer, without Carpenters, Smiths, Bricklayers and other Trades Men, and even without men capable of doing any work it is impossible to proceed with them in making this Settlement." In view of all these problems already besetting the enterprise, Barnwell, well-seasoned in South Carolinan politics, suggested the Governor consult the Council and see "how far this Province is able to supply these wants, and propose the same to the General Assembly".

In the interim, Barnwell proposed that "30 of the Scout Men now in the Country's pay at Port Royal ... go immediately and secure the possession of that place by a small Palisado Fort and a few Huts, until measures can be concerted for making a firm establishment there, and that a sloop or other decked vessel may be procured to attend them and making a Draught Plan of the river and harbour, purely out of the respect I have for the many signal favours bestowed on me by Yr Excellency, having no other way to express my gratitude".

Barnwell ended the "memorial" by pointing out rather succinctly that he found he was getting less than a reasonable salary for his pains, that the promised rank and pay ("the Lieutenancy of the [garrison] upon the same foot with Annapolis Royal and Placentia") was not forthcoming and that he needed some leave "to provide for my private affairs which are in great disorder by my tedious absence from them". (5) Barnwell had indeed been away from his Port Royal plantations and Charles Town obligations for over a year, so his request was scarcely surprising.

The Governor, however, was anxious not to lose momentum on the Fort issue. On the same day, 3rd June, 1721, "His Excellency acquainted the Council of his Majesty's design of building a fort and settlement on the Altamaha River, and proposed to them to name a proper person to have the direction of the same, who agreeing that

Col. John Barnwell was the most proper person, It was ordered that the said Mr. Barnwell do prepare and lay before this Board on Wednesday next for their consideration, by what methods he proposed to carry on and effect the said Settlement and what instructions he shall think may be necessary to be given him for that purpose." (6)

By 7th June, the Council had considered what Barnwell proposed in a "memorial relative to the settling a fort on the Allatamaha [sic] River" (7) and resolved to leave "the entire building and settling" of the Fort to Barnwell and instructed him to do so "without loss of time". By the following day, Barnwell had compiled and placed all the necessary requisitions and instructions before Council members. After some amendments, the Council approved his whole undertaking. Accordingly, Governor Nicholson issued a string of written orders on 9th June, 1721, to the requisite authorities in Charles Town and at Port Royal to provide "Coll. John Barnwell who is Commissioned to take possession of the Alamaha [sic] River all and singular such Ordinances Stores Tools and other necessaries, he shall time to time require of you for His Majesties Service together with the Two Jack Flaggs Speaking Trumpet prospective Glass Lanthorns or any other necessarys ... "

"... Two hundred weight of Muskett powder newly put in-to the Magazine and one hundred weight of Canon powder" were mentioned, along with "four small Field pieces ..." together with "a hundred Ball fitting to the same, wth their Carriages Sponges Ramers Ladels Lin Stocks and other accoutrements belonging to the same". (8)

Barnwell had also made an agreement on 9th June with Jonathan Collings, master and owner of the sloop JONATHAN AND SARAH, to hire the sloop to take him and his men to the "River of St. George, alias Alatamaha", (9) and attend the men while there, for a total cost of Carolina pounds 40. (10)

Chapter Four

Building the Fort

John Barnwell's feverish activities to get equipped, loaded and away sound all too familiar. As he recounts at the beginning of his July, 1721, Journal-report to Governor Nicholson, "I must acquaint You with how many Difficulties I mett with before I left Port Royall -

"From the 16th of June to the 6th July there did not pass One day without Rain. So that it was with great difficulty I could gett Beeff or Pork the woods being all rotten & underwater that the hunters mett with bad Success and dayly fell Sick of ffluxes and Agues, and ffurther Some busie people had put Strange notions into the Scoutmen, that I was affraid of their Running away with the Boats.

"Now These Scoutmen are a wild Idle people & Continually Sotting if they can gett any Rum for Trust or money. Yet they are greatly useful for Such Expeditions as these if well & Tenderly managed, ffor as their Chiefest Imploy is to hunt the fforest or ffish, So there is Scarce One of Them but understands the Hoe, the Axe, the Saw, as well as their Gun and Oar -

"These people finding the publick Imploy an Idle life where They found provisions, and their wages finds them in Rum Chosed it rather than the Trades they were brought up in.

"And Since I went to England, they have intirely lost the

litle Discipline they had, and being Every One in Debt, and having no Dependence on anything in this Province, are ready for the Run on the least disgust, So you may now Guess what hopefull fellows I have to deal with to begin a new Settlement ... " (1)

Barnwell finally managed to get 26 able-bodied Scoutmen to accompany him. He was not so lucky with the six Creek Indians who reneged on their promises to go south to the Altamaha River with him. He eventually secured the services of a Tuskarora and another Creek Indian, whilst refusing other Edisto and Tuskarora Indians' offers for fear of their latent antipathies.

He continued his account in rueful fashion: "Thus on Thursday the 6th of July, I furnished my Self with all Such Necessary's as I wanted out of the Kings Store at Beaufort and took Every thing belonging to the Port Royalle Scout, and putt them on Board the Sloop, the Whale Boat and my perriaugoe, which with that & ye provisions were deep loaded, and having hired One David Duvall & his two Slaves which are Sawyers, I sent him in the Whale Boat to take Charge of her, & by much ado gott away that night, the men all drunk as beasts, and fell down 3 miles & rested that Night.

"I was in Good health when I left Beaufort, But one of the men pretending to carry me into my Boat, fell down with me & duck'd me, over head in ye water/ I not perceiving he was drunk, till it was too late, & unwilling to go ashore again to dry myself least the men Should disperse & run away, I lay all night wett, my linnen being on Board the Sloop, So it caused my Sickness to Return So Violent, that I was once determined to Return, if I had mett the Sloop according to appointment, But before I mett her, I was mended, & thank God am now in good health." (2)

Barnwell left on July 7th and with Captain Palmeter and seven of his men and his boat, proceeded within land, to the mouth of the Savannah River. He reached the northernmost mouth of the Altamaha River at night on

July 11th, having missed his rendezvous with the sloop. The next morning, he decided to go on to the place he had picked for the settlement and unload before looking for the sloop. "So I took a fair and wide Strait Branch of the River which going in a West Course for 15 mile among prodigious fresh water Marshes resembling Meadows, and subdividing itself into great Arms & smaller branches that meeting again in the Sound makes them Islands; at last coming to the woods I was perplex'd to find nothing but vast Cypress Swamps reaching many miles; I followed the Northwest Branch, which is ye broadest Branch, about 4 mile, and then I discovered a Branch going North, which perceiving the Ebb making that way I was looking for, and there I knew a very high Bluff, and rested that night." A survey map of the "Mouth of the Alatamahaw River with the Adjacent lands" is attributed today to John Barnwell and shows Fort King George as it was later sited, as well as two roads to the "Palachicolas" and "Okanees". (3)

On July 13th, he "ordered the People to Row 3 miles down to this pleasant point, where they unloaded the boats, and pitched the four Tents I brought with me, and The / Indians field being grown up with Small Bushes, they Set The Same on fire and Cleared a good way Round". He later met up with the sloop and brought her to "an Anchor before this point, and made all the men Merry drinking His Majesty's and Your Excellency's health". (4)

The real work started early next morning. Barnwell first had the "great Guns" unloaded and mounted. He was not taking any chances, since everyone was concerned lest any enemy discover them before the fort was constructed. Then he "gott the mill, the grindstone, and the Smiths or Armorers tools up, Some grinding the Tools, others helving the Axes & ctra and in Short made a good dayes work". Next day, some men set and filed whip saws and crosscut saws, while others were sent to the cypress swamps for bark for the mens' huts. They got three huts constructed that same day.

Things began to deteriorate after that. The weather was hot. A "Terrible Thunder Showr" marooned Barnwell for the night on an island where he had been hunting for venison. He got lost up a branch of the river and he and his men were "reduced to great Extremity. - for all the branches we hitherto went thro, were ffresh water, and we neglected to take any in our Boat, But this proving Salt / Those that toyled at the Oar were ready to faint". Barnwell got them ashore and barbecued the meat lest it spoil. Some of the men later found "thick nasty water" by digging in the sand. To cap it all, when Barnwell eventually got back to the building site, he found the men "had been in a Mutiny about their work".

As he explained to the Governor, "Now there being no wood or Timber, within Three miles of this it was impracticable to build any thing of a Redoubt or Small ffort but with plank, and the most Convenient place for Cypruss is also 3 miles off. This Cypruss can't be gott out of the Swamp without wading naked up to the waist or Sometimes to the neck, which is a Terrible Slavery, and Especially now in the dog days, when Musketos are in their Vigour ... " (5)

Barnwell decided that he had no choice but to pay the Scoutmen to do this heavy work for they were his sole resource, other than two of his own slaves he had brought along as sawyers, together with Mr. Duvall's two slave sawyers.

On 18th July, he called all the men together and told them he was going to build a "Redoubt like a Logg House; that in order to do it I should want 100 pieces of Cypruss, that would Square a foot at least and 12 feet long". Barnwell offered them 15 shillings' extra pay to deliver such lumber to the sawpit. Thirteen men volunteered and that day produced seven such logs. He then contracted with three white sawyers and another of his slaves to "Saw 4 Inch plank [which I found muskett proof]" and agreed on wages with the carpenters and shinglers. Barnwell was being thorough - he also had the armourer "View and Clean all the arms, and mend what was amiss, gott Partridg bags for the great Guns & ctra, and had live oak logs cut to ballast the sloop now that it had been unloaded". The sloop's defenceless situation concerned Barnwell and he decided to send her back to Port Royal after sounding the three bars he had found in the river.

By July 21st, he had "a good number of 4 Inch plank Sawed", so caused "double Stakes to be Sett up at 6 ffeet distance round our Camp, and putt the plank between them ffor a Brest work round until the fframe for the Logg house is ready". Things were going better; men "troubled with agues at Port Royal are recovered here, it is much pleasanter than Port Royal". He described the vast marshes, St. Simons Island's first bluff at least 12 miles away, the Indian fields to the west and "at the very point where we are, is a lovely knott of live Oak Trees, without whose Shade it had been very troublesome Settling here". (6)

He prevailed on Capt. Palmeter to stay on until October and hired Mr. Duvall and his two slaves for three months, explaining, "Tho he is not Excellent at no One thing, yett he is handy at a great many things, I made him Storekeeper, & he bleeds & gives physick, and he handles the Ax and what not..." "As for Mr. Ballantyn the Armourer," he continued, "I could not do without him by reason he fixed our Tools and Arms..."

He continued the Journal to the Governor by saying he had been as diligent, cautious and economical as if he had been acting on his own account. Barnwell added, "If This place be not thought the properest place for the Security of the River, But that it must be removed to the Island of St. Simons, there will be nothing lost, for this Cypruss plank is valuable & Sliding the plank into the frame in Chanels made on purpose without nailing or tronelling, it may in a day be taken to pieces & putt up again without the least damage." (7) He ended by saying he was keenly aware of Spanish St. Augustine being only 90 miles to the south, but hoped that the fort's position on the mainland would preclude it being discovered before it was secure against all attack save cannon. Barnwell intended to send his Journal to the Governor at an early date, but when he used the "Pilote Boat and my perriaugoe" to sound the bars and estimated four days for the job, he ran into problems. "But to my great vexation, that now being Eight days about it, I am almost as much to Seek as ever, whether it proceeds from the unskilfulness or timourousness or Both of the pilote Collings, I am at a loss to know, being myself but little versed in working a Sloop or any other vessell ..." Barnwell was learning more about the serpentine un-predictabilities of the marshland world, compounded by summer thunderstorms. However, he was able to report, "I have searched every Corner for 20 miles round ffrom the Sea, & have not discovered any Bluff or ffirm land on the main but this place at the Garrison point and on the Same branch above it". (8)

When Capt. Collings, John Ballantyn (the Armourer) and David Duvall (the Storekeeper) returned to Charles Town on 3rd August, 1721, with John Barnwell's account of the first days at the Fort, they were all requested to attend the Lower House. The Members were eager to have firsthand accounts of all that had transpired. The Governor was obviously satisfied with Barnwell's progress for he urged the Lower House to send the provisions and other necessaries Barnwell required as soon as possible. The House replied on August 5th with the first hints of future wrangling over who should pay for the construction and maintenance of the Fort - the King or the Province of South Carolina.

The South Carolina Legislative Journals for August, 1721, reflect the difficulties the Governor had in finding men to send south to Barnwell, while the soldiers of the Independent Company were still unfit for service. He had to juggle men around the various garrisons and reconcile the different expenses to be met by South Carolina itself and by London, whilst recognising that the Fort on the Altamaha River was neither secured nor settled as yet. In a letter received by the Governor on 21st August, 1721, Barnwell stated, "This day I am promised the assistance of some of the soldiers to get the Timber together that is to build their Barracks. It proves very sickly among my Scoutmen there being one dead this morning and another just upon point of death, and ten more sick for we have had scarce a dry day since I came up. The Woods are full of water and the men going backward and forward and killing Beef and out day and night as well as they are seasoned can't bear so much well ... this strange sort of weather has occasioned my thus long delaying never having one good day's work done." (9)

Pay rates for the different men destined for the "Altamaha Fort" loom large in the minutes of House deliberations. Fifteen pounds a month were allowed for "an able surgeon". Six pounds a month, plus 40 shillings extra per month, was the pay offered for "as many of the prisoners lately arrived from the Havanah as are willing to enlist themselves to serve at the Alatamaha Fort" (on 13th August, 1721). Lieutenant Haynes and his men at the Savannah garrison (or Fort Moore as the trading post on the north bank of the Savannah River was later named) should be sent to the new Fort and for the "Extraordinary services they shall do at the ... new fort they shall be allowed over and above 40 shillings a month". A tone of impatience was also creeping into the House minutes. Evidently the Altamaha Fort was already getting a bad name among servicemen. Captain Munger was instructed to remind any protesting Highlander "late servants to the public" (10) that the Governor would not countenance their making difficulties about going to the Fort since they had already had three years of service remitted.

The inducements seemed to work, for on 14th August, 1721, Alexander Parris, Public Receiver, was ordered to advance a month's pay to five men enlisted for the "new settlement at the Altamaha River". Doctor William Dalzell who lived at James Kinloch's was hired on 25th August to be surgeon at the Fort. Meanwhile, Indian agent Colonel Theophilus Hastings was proposing to the House that he "bring down and settle a number of Creek Indians, with their families, at the Alatamaha Fort". Secretary Hart suggested to the House that the "said Hastings have the said trade to himself or his assigns for three years to come with the said Creek Indians, that shall settle within twenty miles, or come to trade in that compass round the said fort..." Hart stipulated, "That the Indians to the number of 100 men and their families, shall by the said Hastings means come to hunt, and settle near the said Altamaha settlement, and shall settle their wives and children within a quarter of a mile of the said fort, to be under the command of the guns thereof as hostages for their abiding there". (11) Hastings was to trade with the Indians at rates current among traders, and if the Indians would not trade, then they would be forced to move away.

Barnwell, meanwhile, was writing to the Governor on September 11th, and delivering a report in person to the House on 16th September. He probably brought back to Charles Town with him the map he had prepared "For His Excellency General Nicholson by his Sert. J. Barnwell" on August 29th, 1721, on "The Northern B(ran)ch of Alatama River which joyns ye main River 5 miles higher up ..." A drawing of the "Alatama plank'd house" appears on the map and has a rather lengthy legend. On the map, it is located at a fork at which a creek empties into the main river channel. There are many explanatory legends about the terrain, the marshes and previous Indian settlements. He wrote, for example, "Ten acre field, sandy, good for potatoes, left by the Huspaw People (belonging to the Yemassees) when they heard in 1715 that the English were coming to attack them."

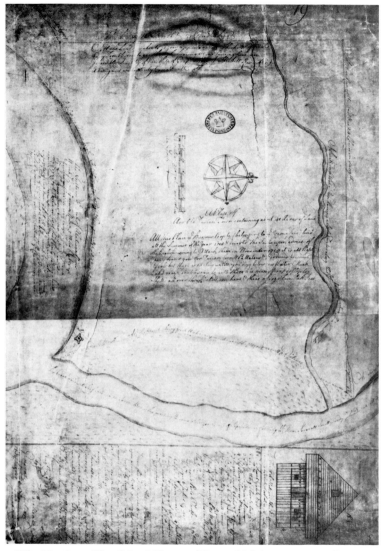

"The Northern B[ran]ch of Alatama River which joyns ye main River 5
miles higher up … August 29th, 1721. For his Excellency General
Nicholson by his Sert. J. Barnwell." The "Alatama plank'd house" is
shown, together with explanatory legends about Indian settlement,
the terrain and water.
(Map courtesy of Hargrett Rare Book and Manuscript Library,
University of Georgia)

Barnwell also brought back to Charles Town the Chart he had prepared on September 2nd of St. Simons Harbour, made after he sounded the bars out from the mouth of the Altamaha River. (12)

After hearing these reports and receiving complaints from other sources about the state of the various garrisons at the Province's charge, the House notified the Governor of its Resolutiuon to enlarge the Fort "at Alatamaha River". They decided to make it "sufficient for your Excellency's whole Independent Company, and for 20 men of the Scoutmen to continue with them, to be employed in scouting, hunting, fishing and planting, and also to engage with them by their former acquaintance as many of our friendly Indians to assist them, therein the same, until his Majesty's forces are better acquainted with the methods of living in this country". (13) Barnwell's shrewd common sense comes through this resolution - the House obviously respected his tough realism. In the interim, the Port Royal barracks were to be repaired. The men quartered there could neither defend themselves against weather nor enemy, declared the House. The Governor agreed, for he was also concerned about the men's well being and the barracks' defences.

On this visit to Charles Town, there is the first hint of Barnwell having possibly overtaxed himself in his Altamaha Fort venture. A petition dated 16th September, 1721, from John Barnwell reads, "having for the space of 20 months last served the public of this Province with utmost application whereby he has suffered very much in his private affairs, therefore prays to be allowed to retire to his family, discharging him from all such offices as may interfere with the same". (14) Not only did Barnwell, his wife Ann Berners, their two sons and six daughters own and manage extensive plantations, but Barnwell himself was still a leading member of the Assembly. He had also been appointed to the first Committee of Correspondence liaising with the Government in London. The Altamaha Fort probably had proved far more demanding an undertaking than John Barnwell desired.

Barnwell's petition to retire from public office was greeted with a statement from the Governor verging on panic - "We ... recommend to you as a thing of the utmost consequence to the Province that you will think of some way to gratify the said Col. Barnwell for his care, trouble, and hazard in erecting the fort ... & ... We being of the opinion if he should decline returning thither, what has already been done will be rendered useless, and may endanger the lives of his Majesty's subjects there for want of a proper person to command them ..." (15) The upshot of this was an extra allowance of 10 shillings a day to Barnwell until the engineer, who still had not come out from England, should arrive.

By 20th September, John Barnwell seemed back in harness, suggesting that the Altamaha Fort be enlarged and removed to St. Simons Island and that barracks be constructed for 100 men and their officers. This idea was speedily rejected and the House suggested Barnwell be commissioned Engineer to replace the missing engineer from England. A name for the Fort was also requested. The reply came the same day - FORT KING GEORGE. Barnwell was not yet commissioned Engineer, but the Governor specified he finish the redoubt, build barracks for the men and provide a "draught of the harbour, River and St. Simons Island with the fort he proposes to build thereon..." without moving the existing fort to St. Simons. (16)

The Governor ended this exchange between himself and the House by announcing on 21st September his intention to commission Col. Barnwell Engineer and Commander in Chief of King George's Fort at "Allatamaha". A Lieutenant, an Ensign, 2 sergeants, 2 corporals and a drum were ordered sent by periagua to Fort King George, along with necessary provisions.

Chapter Five

An Expensive Venture

In October, 1721, the building of Fort King George was apparently completed. It was "a planked house", or gabled blockhouse, twenty-six feet square. There were three floors: a magazine floor, a gunfloor at six feet from the ground, with walls pierced for cannon and musketry, and above, a "jetting floor to clear the sides", with more loopholes for small arms. High in the gable, a lookout window commanded a wide view of river, marsh and old Indian fields, with St. Simons Island to the east and southeast. On the land side, the blockhouse was defended by an earthen parapet, five to six feet high, with a bastion, surrounding palisades and a moat. Another parapet of fascines fronted the river, and the palisades were continued along the marsh on the northeast side. Within this irregular triangle, in a space measuring two hundred by three hundred feet, stood several palmetto-roofed huts and barracks. (1)

By January, 1722, an Engineer, Capt. John Barker, had joined the Fort, and there was talk of surveying a possible road between Alatamaha and Fort Moore and thence to Congaree Fort. The Lower House again sent messages to the Governor and Council in February about the Province's

View over the north branch of the Darien River and marsh from
Fort King George during reconstruction
(Photograph courtesy of Georgia Department of Natural Resources)

difficulty in paying for the constructed Fort and its inability to afford any additional buildings. The Governor had specified "a store-house for six months provisions, barracks with chimneys, and a guard room for the centinels, another for the sergeants, corporals, drummers. Four Commission officers barracks. An hospital for the sick and a room for the surgeon. A place for a chapel and a room for the chaplain. A storehouse for ordnance stores, a magazine for powder and a room for an engineer. A room for a public kitchen and for baking and brewing. These buildings to be made in the form of a square for a parade in the middle."

The Governor suggested that if the Assembly could not finance these additional buildings, they could perhaps

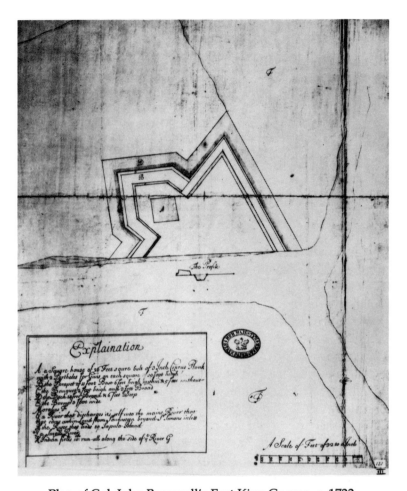

Plan of Col. John Barnwell's Fort King George, c. 1722,
by an unknown pen
(Map courtesy of Hargrett Rare Book and Manuscript Library,
University of Georgia)

enlarge the present Fort to accommodate 50-60 men until the King's decision about erecting a fort on St. Simons Island be known. He also recommended the make-up of any Independent Company recruited to be :

> "Sergeants   3
> Corporals   4
> Besides commissioned officers -
> Drummers   2
> Centinels   <u>100</u>
>   109 " (2)

In reply, the House pointed out that according to Capt. Barker, "the fort already built there is sufficient to answer that design. And as there is a strong house of 26 feet square built, whose lower rooms being already divided into three partitions, is of capacity not only to hold eight or nine months provisions for 100 men, but also to preserve as much ordnance stores as that garrison may have occasion for. That as the middle floor of the said house has only two great guns mounted in it, it may conveniently serve as a guard room in summer and upon occasion may accommodate the Common Officers who have not families in the summer very well. And the barracks that are ordered to be transported to that fort - being ninety feet long and fourteen feet wide when finished - will be more than sufficient to contain the number of your Excellency's Company proposed for garrisoning that place." (3) The House went on to say that a man on the spot was a bricklayer, so he could make all the materials needed for ovens and chimneys, thereby saving some money.

The expenses incurred by Fort King George were already so great, the House members felt, that the only way to meet these and other "contingent charges of this government" was to increase taxes. And that, "we are afraid will so affect several industrious planters as may oblige them to desert the Province". The Governor thus got no help at all from the House in his list of requirements. Clearly he saw a much larger role for the Fort than did the House by that time; they were more concerned about cutting costs. During the 1720s, there were constant struggles between the Assembly, the Council and the Governor over issuing paper money to tide the Province over while the Treasury was empty between tax bills. The earlier Indian wars had practically bankrupted South Carolina. "We are just now the poorest Colony in all America, and have both appearances of ruine," lamented a Carolinian in 1718. (4) So Fort King George was understandably just one of the items to sacrifice whenever possible in the provincial budget.

By February 17th, 1722, the House was backing out of any agreement to allow Barnwell a salary as Governor and Commander in Chief of Fort King George. Members were obviously concerned by this time about the Fort's defensive capabilities, its building requirements and the continued expensive use of scout boats along the coast. They appointed a Committee to investigate the situation. This Committee reported, "That the fortifications of Fort King George are in so good a posture of defence that with the expence of 1 hhd (hogshead) of rum, some sugar and tobacco, which the present command there demands and engages to complete the fortifications therewith, will be able to make a long defence against a powerful enemy with 50 men, provided they have provisions and ammunition sufficient ...

"That it is the opinion of the Committee that as soon as the barracks built and framed by Capt. Grey at Beaufort are transported to Fort King George and there finished in order to receive his Excellency's whole Independent Company that then the said Company will be in sufficient garrison for that place without having there any men in the country's pay..." The Commission expressed concern

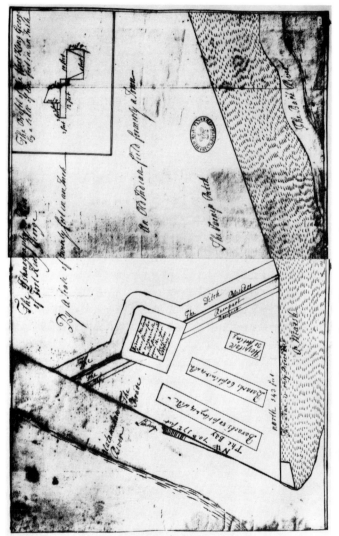

The Ishnography or plan of Fort King George c. 1722. Inset is the "Profil of the Fort King George by a scale of ten feet in an inch". (Map courtesy of Georgia Department of Archives and History)

about the poor victualling situation at the fort and advised the Governor to "press" his contractors on the matter. The Commissioners recommended that Col. Barnwell be released, as from 25th March, of his obligations since he had fulfilled the "designs of the General Assembly" as well as possible.

They ended by stating that "it is of the opinion of the Committee that notwithstanding what Capt. Barker his Majesty's engineer offers to the contrary, that a fort built on St. Simons Island would be of great advantage to the Province for securing a good harbour, stopping the Water Passage, and keep entirely the possession of the River Altamaha, and that it be accordingly represented to his Majesty as also how unable this Province is to undertake a work of that charge". (5)

The Committee, whose report was signed by John Woodward, Capt. Wm. Bull, Benj'm Schenking(s), John Raven, Indian Commissioner and merchant Charles Hill, Indian Commissioner and Colonel George Chicken and Indian Commissioner and Major John Fenwick, examined the whole situation exhaustively. They recommended that the House reconsider Barnwell's salary situation. Another recommendation was that one of the Lieutenants at the Fort, Lt. Joseph Lambert ("a good, honest man" according to Governor Nicholson (6)), be recompensed for the loss of "most of his goods by those that run away with the public periagua". They also suggested that Capt. Grey's accounts for the barracks' construction be verified as they seemed very high. Lt. Lambert was eventually paid 200 pounds for his "sufferings and losses" - history does not relate whether the thieves were caught or the public periagua recovered.

Chapter Six

Spanish Manoeuvers

At the end of February, 1722, the Governor and House members all became very concerned at a new development. In what was seen as a ploy to take "a survey of the country" (including the recently completed Fort King George) and stir up trouble among the Creek Indians and the slaves in South Carolina, Don Antonio de Benavides, Spanish Governor of St. Augustine, sent a letter via Don Francisco Menendez Márques, to Governor Nicholson. Don Francisco was accompanied by 27-30 men, and their route had taken them through the "heart of our country, through all our inlets and settlements, and more especially at a time when they declare they have no certain and direct advice of the conclusion of a peace", as the House pointed out. (1)

The construction of Fort King George by the British had, in truth, represented "a flagrant intrusion into ancient Spanish territory. A generation had passed since mission bells had sounded over the Bocas de Talaje, but Spain had never yielded title to Guale. Barnwell, hunting for Spanish figs and garlic among the ruins of Zapala (Sapelo Island) and Asao (a mission on St. Simons Island), had grounds for fearing Spanish opposition to his adventure; indeed, he fixed upon the more sheltered mainland rather than St. Simons for just that reason." (2) Benavides and his Spanish

Floridians were not only harassed by Indian raids incited by the British, but Benavides had learned, too late, of this invasion of Spanish lands by the builders of the Fort. "Challenging France, Barnwell and his backers had provoked another contest with Spain for Guale, a contest in diplomacy and war which continued until 1763." (3)

Don Francisco Menendez Márques was instructed to settle by treaty all matters of territory, partisan warfare, runaway slaves and Spanish prisoners. Nicholson side-stepped all the issues with righteous indignation and replied that he had no authority to negotiate a treaty. To the charge of a "New Settlement" on the Altamaha, the Governor retorted that the Fort was built under Royal orders "for the better Securing of those his Majesty's dominions". (4)

The Spanish tarried in Charles Town and negotiations were at a standstill. To add insult to injury, the South Carolinians had to pay all expenses for their unwanted guests. In their haste to get rid of the Spaniards, the House members urged the Governor to send them back to St. Augustine any way he saw fit but not "in the sloop designed for Alatamaha", for they "ought not to return within land in the manner they came". (5) The Inland Waterway, already in use by the scout boats to and from Fort King George, was strategically too sensitive to let the Spaniards learn any more about it.

The Governor, Council and Assembly finally gathered in mid-March to bid farewell to the Spanish, after peace was "concluded" with them, and toasts drunk to the health of His Majesty and His Catholic Majesty. The British, however, were not taking any chances : for a fee of Carolina pounds 57.17, John Barnwell was appointed to escort the Spanish under a flag of truce from Port Royal to St. Simons with a scout boat, with check points set up at Stone Bridge and Dawhoe. The Governor also suggested "some of the country men and Indians" be left at Fort King George "to scout about both by land and water for fear of any surprises". (6)

The British proved correct in their suspicion that this had been a trouble-making expedition on the Spaniards' part. By May, 1722, Charles Town was full of rumours of impending Spanish attacks on Fort King George. The House feared "that the men now left of your Excellency's Company will not be able to maintain that fort against such a body of men as we may reasonably expect will attempt the reducing of it". Reinforcements were needed from England, but their cost would have to be met eventually by the Crown. Meanwhile the House members suggested Captain William Martin, commanding HMS BLANDFORD out of Virginia, be requested to cruise between St. Augustine and Port Royal "in case an attack may happen", to reinforce the scout boats. (7) The Yemassee Indians were also stirring again in support of the Spanish, supposedly against Fort King George. In June, Colonel Theophilus Hastings, the Indian trader, was directed to try to get them "to submit to Carolina" and if they refused, he was empowered to capture every Yemassee over the age of 10 and be paid 50 pounds a head for these new slaves. Otherwise, he was "to engage the Creeks or any other Indians to utterly destroy the said nation of Yemassees," for which he would receive 1000 pounds. (8)

Finally, in a letter of December 20th, 1722, Messrs. Chetwynd, Dominique, Pelham and Bladen of the London Board of Trade wrote to the King in response to a letter transmitted from him : "We have considered the complaint of the Spanish Ambassador, relating to the new Fort lately built at the Tomoia and the mouths of ye Talaje, by which we presume the Sd. Ambassador means the Fort lately erected by your Majesty's Orders at ye embouchure of the Alatamaha. Whereon we humbly beg leave to represent to your Majesty :

"That in the year 1720, your Majesty having received complaints of great Disorders in South Carolina, was graciously pleased to resume ye Government of that

Province, and to constitute Col. Nicholson Govr thereof, for your Majesty. Upon which occasion this Board having duly considered the State of that Province, which is the South Frontier of your Majesty's Dominion on the Continent of America, did humbly conceive it might be necessary, in order to prevent further encroachments from the subjects of the French or Spanish nation, as well as to secure the navigation of the Alatamaha River, that a fort should be built at the mouth of the said River, and we are very much surprized that the Spanish Ambassador should make any complaint thereof, because the Land where the sd Fort is built is certainly a part of your Majesty's Province of South Carolina, to which your Majesty has a most undoubted Title, and if it should be thought necessary to enter further into the discussion of this matter, we shall be ready to furnish sufficient Proofs to verify the Same." (9)

The Spanish did not desist. Lieutenant Charles Huddy (commissioned in November, 1722, and obviously zealous in performing his duties), wrote from Fort King George on 9th February, 1723, to say, "On the 7th inst. arrived here a boat from St. Augustine with 6 men with their arms and a flagg of truice [sic] the Head man declaring himself to be a Lieutenant, that on my demanding to see his commission he said he had left it at St. Augustine. Two of them would have stayed here, and swore they would never more serve the King of Spain. They differing among themselves the head man of them told me at first 'twas his master's orders, the first boat he met to deliver the enclosed letter for your Excellency and immediately to return, but on examination of them separately they disagreed on their stories, as Capt. Parmeter will inform you, and my diligence in securing of them and their boat persuant to my instructions, vizt. No. 41: 'You are upon no account whatever to keep and correspondence with the French or Spaniards or deal, trade or traffic with them, and if any of them come to your garrison under any pretense whatever you are to apprehend them and keep them close prisoners until you can send them to his Excellency'." (10)

Capt. Parmeter accompanied his prisoners to Charles Town and more fuel was added to the Spanish fire. Indeed, the Governor was already urging that "a Committee of both houses may consider of what is proper to be done in case the Governor of St. Augustine should send hither as he has done twice already ... " (11)

The Spanish would continue to cause problems, directly or via their Yemassee friends, for many a year ahead.

Chapter Seven

Accounts and Recruits

Meanwhile, life continued busily at Fort King George with the usual quota of difficulties. Captain John Barker, His Majesty's Engineer, wrote on March 20th, 1722, to say ill health and his age precluded him from continuing to work at the Fort. The House was skeptical of this reason, telling the Governor, "you may see his inability or un-willingness to perform his duty in seeing the fortifications and barracks at Fort King George finished and his desire of leave to stay here" (1) in Charles Town. Since Barker had obviously had enough of the hardships at the Fort, Barnwell was recommended as the "proper person" to finish the work at the Fort.

The House needed an accounting of expenditures for the Fort. On 19th June, 1722, they recorded : "As to what relates to the charges this Province has been at, and at what further may be necessary to be expended or furnished for the Fort King George it is the opinion of the committee that Col. John Barnwell who has been long employed by the government in that affair, be ordered to prepare an estimate of the same, making a distinction of the extraordinary charge of the said Fort separate from the charge this government was at, about maintaining the scout boats which last expence this government would be out if this Fort had never been erected".

The House wanted to present London with the accounts for reimbursement. They also intended to ask for reinforcements for the garrison at Fort King George and for a considerable land grant on the Altamaha River for a town and settlement. They were hoping, too, that a better fort would be built on St. Simons Island to protect that harbour. (2) They were also trying to encourage Barnwell to settle permanently at the new Altamaha settlement by finally recommending him to be Governor or Lieutenant Governor. (3)

By November 24th of that year, John Barnwell complied by presenting "An account of the charges and dis-bursements in building a Fort on the River Altamaha in South Carolina by order of Francis Nicholson Esq. Governor of the said Province in persuance of warrant to him for that purpose from their Excellencys the Lords Justices of England, bearing date the 25th day of October 1720.

Vizt.

"To the hire of a Sloop to carry the men & attend them while there   40: -:-
To the pay of 60 men 430 days at 6 pr. diem   645: -:10-
To 2 pr of sawyers 287 days at 3 pr. diem   173: -: 4-
To hire of boats & other Contingencies   11: -:14-
To Col. Barnwell as Engineer and overseer of the works the Engineer being left behind until Capt. Barker came 180 days at 10/   90: -:-

<hr>

                                                 960: -:8-
Errors excepted

                                        John Barnwell." (4)

A further Treasury account mentioned 106 pounds, 6 shillings, and 8 pence for guns, cartridges and sundry

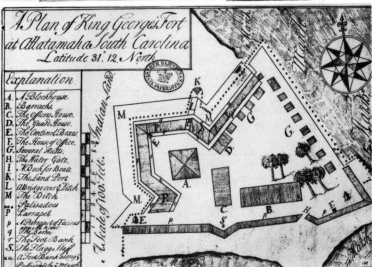

A Plan of King George's Fort at Allatamaha, South Carolina
Latitude 31° 12" North. 1722.
Above are the colours of the Swiss Company.
(Map courtesy of Georgia Department of Archives and History)

other things furnished to His Majesty's Fort King George.

The total amount the Province had already spent at Fort King George was calculated to be 3,162.18 Carolina pounds with 1,837.02 pounds estimated still to be needed, or about 1000 pounds sterling in total.

On August 6th, 1722, House members resolved that "this House will not be at any further charge or expense about the said fort". Additional expenditures were looming because soldiers were dying in large numbers at the Fort. Forty men had already died in less than a year. (5) However, since apprehensions about the Spanish and French hostile intentions had not abated, the House reluctantly committed itself to advancing money to pay for the newly enlisted men "on credit of the Crown". Arrangements for their recruitment and transport to Fort King George reflected anticipated difficulties, for obviously by this time the Fort had a bad reputation for being an unhealthy post bedevilled by hardships and loneliness. Nonetheless, the situation was urgent for "the French ... are busy ... in making a new settlement called New Orleans" (founded in 1718). If "more men are not sent to keep the possession of the River Allatamaha before the 1st of March next the same will be deserted and we have reason to believe that the Spaniards or French will not neglect so fair an opportunity to take possession thereof." (6)

In their need to find recruits for the Fort, the South Carolinians did not seem to pay too much attention at first to the credentials of a company of "Switzer's" (Swiss) who deserted from the French near the Mississippi and came to Charles Town in September, 1722, in the sloop ST ELIZABETH OF LOUISIANA, under Master Joseph Lowzon. The Carolinian authorities had indeed received a declaration from the "Switzer Company's" Captain. Later, however, Lieutenant Emmenes, in charge of the Fort, received urgent orders that the "Switzers at Fort King George be forthwith disarmed, and their arms secured by

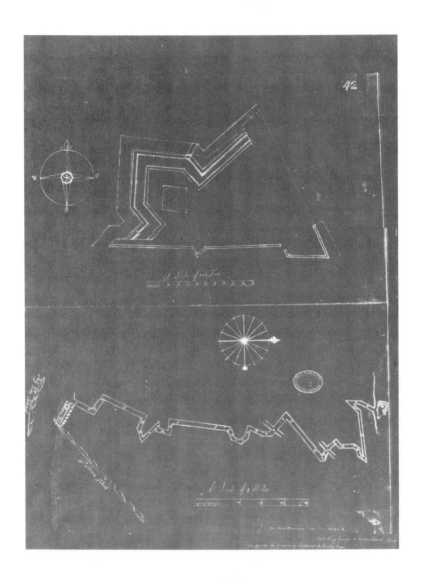

A. Fort King George.
B. Part of St. Simons Island, Georgia. c. 1722
(Map courtesy of Georgia Department of Archives and History)

the Commanding Officer of that fort. That the said Switzers at Fort King George be sent down, but in case there be amongst them any bricklayers, carpenters or smiths, that such of them (as are willing) not exceeding the number of six men, be retained and enlisted into the Independent Company, and the rest of them are at liberty to disperse themselves at Port Royal or any other place within the settlements where they think fit." (7)

An obviously skilled member of this Swiss Company did however leave a permanent record whilst at the Fort. He drew "A Plan of Fort King George at Allatamaha, South Carolina Latitude 31 degrees 12 minutes N". A legend explains the coding system used on the plan to identify the interior structures and the walls. The plan is endorsed, "Carolina. Copy of the colours belonging to the Swiss Company, given them by the Mississippi Company in France. (Reced from Mr. Young Agent for South Carol [ina]) Reced Decr 4th, 1722".

1722 was a busy year at the Fort for map makers. In addition to the Swiss plan, another four Plans extant today are thought to have been made during that year. "A Plan of Fort King George and part of the Altamaha River" shows the fort walls and a portion of the river, with reaches, bearings, distances and soundings noted by its maker, Capt. Stollard, Commander of the Sloop ELIZABETH, sailing between "Fort King George in S. Carolina and St. Simons Island & Barr".

Another document is a two-part plan of the outside wall of the Fort and the outline drawing of St. Simons Island. A third is "the Profil of the ffort King George by a Scale of ten feet in an inch", showing the outer ditch, palisades, ramparts, redoubts, barracks, parade ground and hospital. The fourth plan drawn by an unknown pen in 1722 delineates the outer structure of the Fort as well as surrounding terrain, with an explanatory A - K legend on the bottom of the plan. On a 1726 plan, dock, flagstaff,

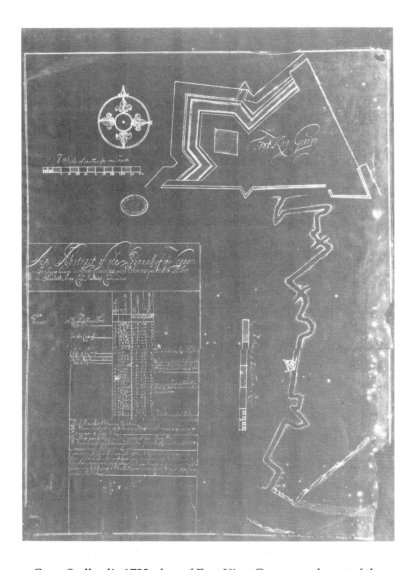

Capt. Stollard's 1722 plan of Fort King George and part of the
river to St. Simons Island and Barr. An inset details reaches,
bearings, distances and soundings, together with sailing
directions from point to point.
(Map courtesy of Georgia Department of Archives and History)

outer defences and gates are shown on a "Plan of Fort King George as it's now Fortifyed". (8)

Lieutenant Emmenes of the Fort, who had had the detail of escorting the first Spanish delegation from St. Augustine to Charles Town, was clearly a conscientious fellow. The House set down in its minutes that "the method Lieut. Emmenes takes in keeping men at Fort King George at work is approved of". (9) He had a great deal to oversee at the Fort. The "Wooden Boxwork or parapet of fascines" at the Fort had already given way and was decaying by September, 1722, thus requiring repair. As Larry E. Ivers, author of 'British Drums on the Southern Frontier' re-marked : "timber and earthen fortifications on the southern frontier required rebuilding every four or five years. Wooden structures and palisades decayed quickly and torrential rains eroded the earthen walls into the moat." (10)

A shed already begun at the Fort and other barracks needed completion. Capt. Palmeter, who had come down with Barnwell in July, 1721, was now storekeeper and quartermaster. He was ordered to keep an account of what meat and provisions the Indians brought in for the garrison and a separate account of what supplies went to anyone other than the soldiers. Provisions for the Fort were a constant problem. Meat could not be salted before October because of the hot weather and supplies of fresh food were unreliable, thus dictating the need always to have "six months salt and dry provisions in the garrison". (11)

Lieutenant Emmenes also had to ensure that if the Creek Indians came to hunt at the garrison, the Cape Fear Indians were to be sent to hunt on the islands. Even with inter-preters, the Lieutenant must have been daunted sometimes by the tasks at this primitive frontier fort where Indians might turn hostile at any moment or the French or Spanish appear on the horizon in overwhelming numbers.

To add to these difficulties, Col. Barnwell, Capt. John Woodward and others reported on 27th September, 1722,

Living history re-enactors portraying the soldiers from His
Majesty's 41st Independent Company
garrisoning Fort King George
(Photograph courtesy of Rundle Cook)

that "several of our people have lately gone a trading up
the Alatamaha River with no other cargo but that of Rum,
Powder and Shott, which trade may in the end prove of
dangerous consequence in creating a misunderstanding
between us and the Indians, when they find that their skins
are disposed of and nothing remains". (12) The Commissioners of the Indian Trade were strongly urged to stop
white men going "among the Indians" and to prevent "the
carrying up of any Rum or other Spirits".

A memorandum to the Governor from the Lower House
on 26th November, 1722, anticipates there "not to be room
for the whole (Independent) Company when it is
thoroughly recruited at Fort King George". Newly arrived
recruits should therefore be sent to another fort, thus
saving money for the Province.

However, the soldiers stationed at Fort King George

were not happy with their lot. Recent arrivals were obviously so horrified at conditions there that many of them deserted. Others were so mutinous, as Ensign Roger Whitley wrote in December, 1722, that they had to be transferred to Captain Martin aboard HMS BLANDFORD as a last resort.

Meanwhile, Colonel Theophilus Hastings was warning Charles Town that "a considerable number of Yemassee Indians were sett out to attack Fort King George". (13) The French and Spanish were up to their old tricks, inciting the Indians to take up arms against the British. Lonely little Fort King George was the obvious easy target. Messages between Charles Town and St. Augustine became more bellicose. Governor Nicholson went as far as to state to the House that "if there should be a war (which God forbid) I hope that his Majesty's garrison at Fort King George, tho so far from the rest of the inhabitants, the forces there and of the country, with Divine assistance, will not only be able to keep it, but to make incursions into the Spanish Government even beyond St. Augustine ..." (14) But the British had to wait another twenty years before they managed to trounce the Spanish at the Battle of Bloody Marsh in 1742 on St. Simons Island.

Names of men stationed at the Fort appear spasmodically through the records. Ensign Bowdler and Dr. Ball made reports about the Fort to the Governor in February, 1722. Ensign Whitley, commissioned in Kensington on 25th June, 1722, had reported on the February, 1723, Spanish visit to Fort King George. He had possibly succeeded Thomas Merryman in his post as Ensign to General Nicholson. Cooper Harris, carpenter Edward Welch, Master Andrew Allen who plied the sloop BETTY to the Fort, a negro carpenter, another negro brick carrier, Dr. John Hutchison, carpenter-sawyer Wm. Almond, carpenter Samuel Crawford, workman Henry Sallas, carpenter Moses Bennett or Thomas Orrack, James Right, Peter Murrey and

William Sladder - deserters and mutineers ... These men have left scant trace of their existence at the Fort.

Other men who served at the Fort are recorded at the time they were commissioned. John Bradfield was commissioned Chaplain on 1st September, 1722, in Kensington to succeed Thomas Hesketh. He in turn was replaced by Edward Dyson, commissioned on 25th March, 1726. John Jeffreyson was commissioned Lieutenant in Kensington on 11th October, 1722, possibly to fill Lieutenant Lambert's place, and he in turn was succeeded by Joseph Eliot who came from a Portsmouth Company of Invalids and was commissioned on 13th March, 1723.

Surgeon Joseph Ball had been commissioned at St. James on 14th February, 1721/22, but seems to have arrived at the Fort in mid-1723, with a possible overlap with another surgeon. In the Paymaster General's accounts was a payment to the Agent K. Eyre of 30 pounds for Surgeon Mason's pay 21 May-17 October, 1723, which implies Mason also practised at Fort King George during Dr. Ball's tenure in 1723. Dr. Ball is later recorded as going on half pay for "American Officers" at the end of 1726, at the age of 50, having served five years in America, "being styled 'Late Surgeon at South Carolina' ". He was succeeded by William Cleland, commissioned on 28th January, 1723/24. Dr. Cleland was replaced, in theory, by Dr. Thomas Cole, commissioned in Kensington on 25th March, 1726. However Dr. Cole apparently did not arrive, so Dr. William Edgar was appointed Surgeon on 21st June, 1726. Ensign John Bowdler went on half pay in May, 1726, at the age of 31, having served nine years in America and the West Indies. He was succeeded by Ensign Philip Delegal who was commissioned on 29th May, 1725, and in 1737 went on from Fort King George and Port Royal to serve in General James Oglethorpe's 42nd Regiment of Foot at Fort Frederica on St. Simons Island. James Watt was also commissioned Lieutenant on 29th April, 1725, in

Kensington, to replace Joseph Elliott who had either retired or died.

1724 proved to be a crucial year for Fort King George's future. Two men pivotal in its development and continued support were no longer living in Charles Town. Brigadier General and Governor Francis Nicholson returned to England in April, 1724, and could thus only play a distant role in South Carolina's affairs after that.

Soon afterwards, his old friend and fort-building ally, Colonel John Barnwell, had to curtail a trip to London because of ill health. He returned home to Charles Town where he died in September, 1724.

Governor Nicholson marked his death by sending a message to the Commons House of Assembly: "Honourable Gentlemen, I am most cordially concerned for the great loss that his Majesty's Province in generall, and more particularly that part to the Southward, hath sustained by the death of the Honourable Colonel Barnwell, and I having been an eye and ear witness of the great service he did for this country, in Great Britain, was in hopes he might have done more." (15)

John Barnwell had put his greatest energies and efforts into the endeavour of establishing Fort King George, ignoring illnesses and tribulations in his drive to accomplish his task. Perhaps if he had lived longer, the fate of Fort King George would have been different.

Meanwhile, life continued at the Fort under the command of Edward Massey who became Captain on 23rd March, 1725/6, with Thomas Farrington commissioned on 15th October, 1726, as his Ensign, succeeding Roger Whitley. Edward Massey was to be a severe critic of conditions prevalent at the Fort, and it was he who finally withdrew his men from their post there. Along with Lieutenants James Watt and Charles Huddy, Ensigns Philip Delegal and Thomas Farrington, Chaplain Edward Dyson and Surgeon William Edgar, Captain Massey was recommissioned by King George II on 20th June, 1727, "in our Province of South Carolina in America", after they had returned to Port Royal in early 1727. (16)

Among the lower ranks, the men left few traces. One soldier did however leave a poignant record of himself. Patrick Martin, a veteran of Britain's regular army who had seen service and known a more refined life in Britain and on the Continent, made out his will at Fort King George on 24th June, 1723, as he lay on his death bed. The will was witnessed by Lieutenant Charles Huddy, Sergeant William Proutting and Dr. Joseph Ball. He declared "IN THE NAME OF GOD AMEN. I Patrick Martin of Fort King George, Soldier, being weak in Body, but of sound and disposing & memory, Praised be God for the same, Do make and declar this my last Will and Testament..." The list of bequests is eloquent.

"Imprimis I do give, devise and bequeath unto Lt. Huddy three yards & a half of holland. Item, I do give, devise and bequeath unto Serjt. Johnson one holland shirt & stock & turn-over..." Falix Mc'anally, Jas. Holmes, Thomas Fitzgerald, Philip Lovett, Michael Kenedy and Robert Knight received shirts, stocks, turn-overs, stockings, shoes and snuffbox. John Carmichael of Charles Town, "my loving friend", was appointed "full and sole Executor". (17) With Patrick Martin's will is an inventory of his personal estate. It included four "wiggs", the holland shirts and turn-overs, a fustian coat, leather breeches and plate buttons, silk stockings ... garments which would have been of more use to Patrick before he came to America than during his last years at primitive Fort King George.

Chapter Eight

The Fort Burns and Spain Impinges

By June, 1724, the South Carolina House Committee on Fort King George was again concerned about the numbers of men stationed there and their victualling. They felt that the Fort should consist of "a Captain, Lieutenant and fifteen men and that the said Garrison be provided with at least four months Provisions and all other necessarys agreeable to these establishments and that they never be without that quantity". (1) All ideas of a planned settlement adjacent to the Fort seem to have evaporated entirely. The Governor and Province were having enough trouble with the Fort itself ...

Then disaster struck. Governor Nicholson had returned to England and Arthur Middleton, President and Commander in Chief of South Carolina, was in charge in Charles Town. His letter of 13th January, 1725/6 to the Governor explains: "I was out of town when the account of the burning of Fort King George came to town, so that I could not give your Excellency so nearly an account of it as otherwise I should have done; the fire began in one of the sergeants' houses, and being covered with palmetto there was no stopping of it, and all the other houses being of wood took fire, and all are consumed, and the walls of the fort being also of wood and much decayed, took fire and burnt down to a very little, so that the poor people are now exposed to the weather, and everything they have; they lost also most of their provisions, but I have taken care to supply them.

"I am in the greatest strait imaginable to know how to get convenient houses and the fort rebuilt, having no power to put workmen to work, or to draw for their pay when the work should be finished. I shall in a few days call the Assembly, and try if they will advance, on the credit of the Government at home, two or three thousand pounds to go on with building again the houses and put the fort in some repair till I can hear from your Excellency, What success I may have in this I can't yet say. You know how that affair stands with the Assembly, but I will do my duty to the best of my power."

Middleton continued by lamenting, "I have had a continual plague and trouble with those people of the Fort ever since your Departure. I here enclose the Lieutenant's original letter, by which you will see how it happened, and how turbulent the soldiers are. The twelve that deserted the garrison and went to St. Augustine I have heard nothing of since. I beg your Excellency will speedily do something in this affair, and that when a new fort shall be built, it may be on the island at the entrance of the river." (2)

By February 7th, Secretary Charles Hart was writing to the Governor about the "unfortunate accident of Fort King George burnt to the ground," saying the House had eventually had to move "to keep possession of that ground, and supply the soldiers with such necessaries to defend them from any sudden surprize of the enemy and the inclemency of the weather. We having more frost and deeper snow than ever I knew since my being here." (3) Middleton also reported that since the House had finally consented to advance 2000 pounds to repair the fort and build barracks, a sloop would be taking "all the necessaries for use intended" (4) to the site. The chief building material was deal, a cheap split-wood product which was relatively flimsy and hardly provided shelter from the extremes of winter and summer.

In September, 1725, Arthur Middleton had to deal once more with the thorny issue of Spanish territorial claims. The Spanish Governor of St. Augustine was again agitating about the boundaries between Florida and South Carolina, especially in view of Fort King George's existence. Because of Spanish trouble-making, not only in Charles Town and London, but among the Creek Indians living along the Altamaha River, Middleton was most apprehensive about King George I being manoeuvered into allowing the Fort to be demolished to satisfy Spanish demands. He felt that, "their being an absolute necessity for the safety of (his Majesty's) subjects that another (fort) be settled on the forks of the (Altamaha) River to maintain that River for we have reason to believe that the Spaniards will erect a fort there as soon as we have quitted possession which will tend to the utter ruin of this colony". (5) He was but echoing the Governor's statement made three years earlier: "I take the affair of Fort King George to be a matter of greatest consequence to this Province." (6)

Meanwhile, things limped along at the Fort. Captain Edward Massey was ordered by the Secretary of War to investigate the cause of the fire and general conditions at the Fort. Once the barracks and fort generally were reconstructed, the men complained ever more bitterly of their condition there. Massey was ordered to the Fort on 19th August, 1726, and submitted his report on 26th April, 1727, on "the unhappy circumstances in which I find my Company now doing duty at Fort King George".

He continued, "The Fort (if a place incapable of defence may be called by that name) is situated 150 miles beyond any settlement and in the most desert part of the province for the security of which or any part of its Trade it might as usefully have been placed in Japan, its whole extent does

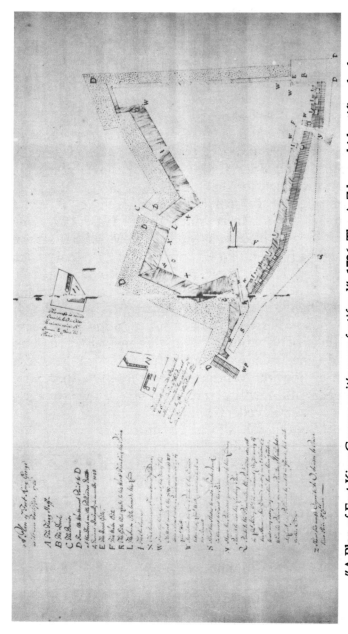

"A Plan of Fort King George as it's now fortifyed", 1726. The A-Z legend identifies dock, flagstaff, outer defences and gates.
(Map courtesy of Georgia Department of Archives and History)

not exceed one third of an Acre, part of it is in a Marsh which renders the Air extremely unwholesome, this joyned to the hard necessity of eating Salt provisions all the year has destroyed great numbers of men of which the death of 4 Commission Officers a surgeon & 130 odd Sergeants and private Centinels in the space of six years, is too fatal proof not to mention the great desertion it has occasioned.

"In this destructive place we are not only destitute of every conveniency and accommodation but labour under the greatest difficulties & heaviest pressures in procuring even Salt provision for the preservation of Life, the great Expence of Carriage making that as well as all other necessaries much dearer than fresh and wholesome provision in the settlements, and as there is but one season for curing the Beef and Pork at which time the whole years store must be laid in, great quantitys of it too frequently corrupt and Stink before it has been six months in the pickle, and what wretched and unwholesome food that which remains must be is not hard to judge after being from Six to Twelve months in Salt, this miserable condition has made the men weary of Life itself and been the occasion of frequent Mutinies and disorders & I am very apprehensive they will desert in a body if they have no hopes of being relieved." (7)

Capt. Massey took aim in no uncertain terms at the President and Assembly of the "Country for whose assistance and relief His Majesty was graciously pleased to raise and pay the company". They "deny Quarters to the Recruits when landed as likewise to any detachment on Service and refuse to supply the Garrison with either Bedding, Fire or Candle ..."

He goes on, "The accommodations in the Fort both for Officers and Soldiers are fit for none but negroes, there are but four small rooms (I should have called them closets) for a Captain, Two Lieutenants, two Ensigns, a Chaplain and a Surgeon, built of thin old Deal only which are no shelter against the excessive heat in summer nor the piercing Winds and cold in Winter, the men are provided for in the same manner but much more closely stowed together, there is but one Chimney in the Garrison, no oven for the men to Bake their Bread, no Fire place to boil their Meat, not so much as a guard house. Cannon indeed I have, but without Ball Rammer or Sponge, for all which I have applied and been refused. Had a nest of pirates been settled where we are I question whether there would have been care taken to distress them so much."

Massey observed wryly, "I find I am not to expect Redress or Assistance from the Country who I firmly believe (some few persons excepted) would sacrifice not only this unfortunate Company but all His Majesty's Forces if in their power could they either save or gain half a score of paltry negroes by it. ...On the Strictest Enquiry I cannot find the late Fort was burnt by design but have reason to suspect the Men were not so active as they might have been in extinquishing the Fire, in hope by the destruction of the Fort they should be delivered from the Miseries they had so long suffered which are inexpressible." (8)

Meanwhile, Indian raids were increasing along the Florida-Carolina border and the Creek nation was causing great concern in Charles Town. " The militia were constantly under arms, plantations were going to wreck, the planters again threatened to desert the most valuable part of the province." (9) In June, 1727, the southern settlers petitioned the Province to transfer the Independent Company from Fort King George to Port Royal for their extra protection.

Fort King George's usefulness was also being challenged by another incident. In July, a trader, Matthew Smallwood, was murdered by a gang of Yemassees and Creeks when he and seven other traders were en route by periagua to their recently-established post at the forks of the Altamaha River. The store was broken open and looted. Three of the traders were taken as prisoners to St.

Augustine, the five others were scalped.

Captain Massey had already urged the Provincial authorities to withdraw his men from the Fort. The Smallwood incident and the threats to the border plantations added weight to his recommendation to the Assembly. A detachment of the Company was already back at Port Royal by 13th March, 1727 (10), for local people were complaining of soldiers trespassing to cut firewood from their lands. Massey then recommended that all the men, cannon, ammunition and stores be withdrawn from Fort King George to Port Royal to defend that place.

Francis Nicholson, still in London, had to handle Massey's report and recommendations. He wrote to the Lords Commissioners for Trade and Plantations to comment on Massey's letter of 26th April, 1727.

In his letter, received on 28th November, 1727, he wrote, "The hardships the Company may have undergone are a natural consequence attending new and remote settlements, but I cannot think they can be so great as represented in the said Captain's letter, and had the officers and soldiers followed my advice and proposals from time to time they might be raising enclosures and making gardens and occasionally have had cattle to supply them with fresh provisions. I did also from time to time send them powder and shot and fishing tackle, there being in that country great plenty of deer, wild fowl and fish and I generally maintained some Indians among them to instruct them in hunting and fishing whereby they might have saved their pay by victualling themselves. ...The sickness of the men is much owing to their being invalids, old, infirm, inactive and Morose, and so lazy and mutinous that could not be prevailed upon to fetch themselves wholesome water as the natives did when they assisted in building the fort and thereby preserved themselves in good health.

"The accommodation for officers and men may probably be bad now, I suppose occasioned by the fire which happened there and burned the fort and reduced it to the state now represented.

"The ammunition and other warlike necessaries for ye said fort I am humbly of opinion should be supplied from ye Board of Ordinance as was done when the Company was first transported thither, which I suppose have been destroyed by ye fire and that an Engineer should be sent over as was then when the said fort was erected to put it in a proper condition and if its situation be not liked to erect one in another place as the engineer shall think fit to answer his late Majesty's intention of securing the property and trade of the said river from the French or Spaniards." (11)

The tone of Nicholson's letter seems resigned and sometimes indignant. Fort King George, in its six years of existence, had caused the Governor innumerable headaches and constant wrangling over finances with the South Carolinians.

Chapter Nine

From Fort to Town Site

Captain Massey's letter, followed by his withdrawal in September, 1727, of the 41st Independent Company of Foot from Fort King George to Port Royal, with all cannon, ammunitions and stores, as approved by the Assembly, was still causing reverberations in London in December that year. Messrs. J. Chetwynd, P. Dominique, T. Pelham, M. Bladen, Edw. Ashe, Oct. Bridgeman and W. Cary of the Board of Trade wrote from Whitehall to George II to outline why Fort King George had been built on the Altamaha River: "to secure that River as being within the Bounds of South Carolina, ...to command the navigation of the said River, which runs up the Country very near to the French settlement on the Mississippi".

They cited Governor Nicholson's letter about the soldiers' continual complaints and commented that the Province had rebuilt the Fort "in a very bad manner. ...Yet we are of opinion that the Fort ought not to be abandoned, ...the reasons being at present rather stronger for maintaining this Fort than they were at First for the erecting of it. This may be done by sending only a Detachment of the Company at Altamaha, for we look upon this Fort at present rather as an Evidence of Your Majesty's Possession than as a Place capable of making any

Living History re-enactors at the reconstructed Fort, the once-
lonely outpost and guardian of South Carolina's southern borders
(Photograph courtesy of Rundle Cook)

considerable Defence." They continued, "we are informed, the Spaniards are equipping several Periaguas to Cruise upon that Coast, and they may probably take possession of this River if not speedily Prevented". (1)

The reply came in form of Instructions to the newly appointed Governor to South Carolina, Robert Johnson: "It is our will and Pleasure, that you do forthwith detach a sufficient number of men from our said Independent Company to keep constant guard at ye said Fort. But if upon enquiry you shall find ye said Fort demolished or you do conceive that a Fort might be erected in any other place more healthful and equally sufficient (for) the Emboucheier and Navigation of Ye River Alatamahama, You are hereby empowered to alter the situation thereof. But in all events You are to take effectual Care that a Fort be repaired or erected ... for securing the navigation of ye said River." (2)

The Lords Commissioners for Trade and Plantations evidently felt they needed more information about the current situation at Fort King George and on 30th May, 1728, they wrote accordingly to Captain John Bowdler in South Carolina. In reply, Captain Bowdler described Fort King George as he knew it to the Lords Commissioners: "The Fort stands upon a branch of the River called Alatamaha and upon a point of land that is very unwholesome and being part of it made ground out of marshy land. In Spring tides, the water flows into the Barracks the Garrison is in Form of a Triangle tho not a just one the two angles to the Land are defended by Mud Walls and a Fosse Pallisaded the other is defended by the River. Captain Barker an engineer sent there by his late Majesty much disapproved of the work and would have persuaded the Government to have demolished it and built it in a more proper place for the services of the country and the health of the soldiers." (3)

Fort King George's fate was virtually sealed by such an assessment. John Barnwell was no longer alive to fight for the Fort. Francis Nicholson had been back in England since 1724. Robert Johnson had only been Governor a short time. Evidently no one else cared as deeply about making a success of the venture as had 'Tuscarora Jack'. By this time, too, South Carolinians were loathe to extend their frontiers southwards to areas where conflict with the Spanish was certain. Their bellicose mood of earlier years had evaporated. The "extremely hard fighting of the Yemassee War, the long discouraging guerrilla war (with the Indians) that followed, financial difficulties, political quarrels and the danger of slave revolts had cooled their aggressive spirit." (4)

However, two sentinels continued to be stationed at Fort King George. One of them, David Alexander, sent a petition to the Council in Charles Town to order his pay and asked "that you will continue him and the other Lookout in the said Service, we thinking of great use to the Publick, and we desire you will likewise order the other Lookout his Pay". (5)

By the late 1720s, London was perhaps more concerned about South Carolina's borders than the colonists themselves. In June, 1730, the Board of Trade instructed Governor Johnson to settle new townships along the rivers in the southern border region, with two of the proposed eleven towns "upon the River Alatamahama". (6) But on the very same day that the Privy Council approved these instructions (September 17th, 1730) (7), the Council referred to the Board of Trade the petition by the Trustees for the charter of the Colony of Georgia. Interestingly, the name for the new colony had been suggested in 1724 by an enterprising promoter, Jean-Pierre Purry of Neuchâtel, Switzerland, for a British frontier settlement scheme for Swiss immigrants on lands south of the Savannah River.

Governor Johnson was also responsible for the maintenance of the forts at Port Royal and Fort King George. Concerned by the constant deterioration of these forts, he investigated building material possibilities and decided "Oyster Shells and Lime" would be much more "durable and Serviceable" (8) than timber. However, the Lower House, when consulted, chose to continue using the cheaper timber for the forts. Even so, by March, 1732/33, Johnson was writing in perplexity to London to say that in vain had he used his "best endeavours to get a Fort and Barracks erected on the River Alatamaha, as I have been commanded by His Majesty, for the reception of a Detachment of His Majesty's Independent Company". The Province had voted about Carolina pounds 4000 for Fort King George and a fort at Port Royal, but despite some timber being sawed and squared for Fort King George, all the money had been spent at Port Royal.

In the meantime, General Oglethorpe, according to the Trustees' plan for the Colony of Georgia, brought the first boatload of settlers to found Savannah in 1733. South Carolina's Assembly promptly concluded that because of the "New Settlers arrival in Georgia," they could "now look upon that place as out of this Province and Government". (9) Buffered by the large new colony, their Province had now shrunk to more manageable proportions. The South Carolinians could thus concentrate on ensuring peace and trade towards the West with a consequent containment of French influences.

Nonetheless, the British flag was still flying over Fort King George in late 1734 when General Oglethorpe returned to England. "The outworks were in ruins" and the two lookouts' existence still depended on "a supply boat's periodic visits". (10) Their duties at the Fort only really ceased in 1736 when Oglethorpe returned to America with a boatload of 177 Scottish Highlanders who came to Barnwell's Bluff, as it was then called, to found Darien. These settlers laid out their town on the high ground above the Altamaha River, "running their lots out to Old Fort King George". (11)

It was thus General Oglethorpe - philanthropist, patriot

and leader of the new Colony of Georgia - who brought to fruition all the endeavours of John Barnwell, Governor Francis Nicholson and London's Board of Trade to ensure Britain's continued sovereignty over the fair lands south of the Savannah River.

The 1733 founding of Savannah, the 1736 settlement of Darien on the Altamaha River and the construction, that same year, of a fort at Frederica on St. Simons Island all represented the culmination of plans espoused by those earlier expansionists to ensure the security of South Carolina's southern frontier. Building and garrisoning Fort King George had been the vital initial stage in the execution of those plans. Fort King George represented the first step towards the colonisation of Georgia and its later statehood.

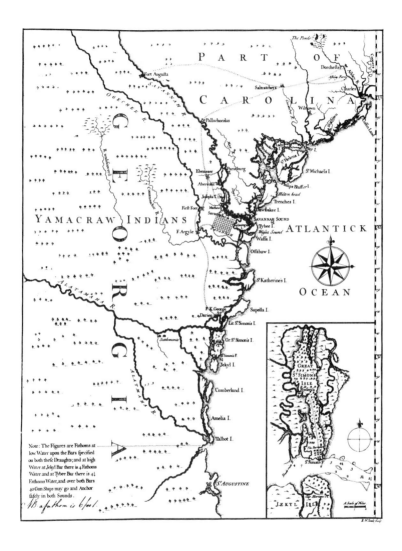

A 1741 map of the Southeast United States, one of the first to
delineate South Carolina and the new colony of Georgia. Both
Fort King George and Darien are clearly marked.
(Map courtesy of Hargrett Rare Book and Manuscript Library,
University of Georgia)

NOTES

Introduction

1. St. Andrew's Parish, 3 August, 1772. Surveyor General Department, Archives & Records Building, Atlanta, Ga. Book C, p. 293
2. William Bartram. Travels in Georgia and Florida. 1773-74. A Report to Dr. John Fothergill. Vol. 1 (Georgia)
3. The Reuben King Journal 1800-1806. Collections of the Georgia Historical Society. Vol XV. Edited by Virginia Steele Wood and Ralph van Wood. 1971
4. Title Deed of sale of Lower Bluff Tract by Sea Island Investments to Georgia State Department of Natural Resources. W.D.10, p. 369
5. Darien News, January 28, 1965

Chapter 1

1. Colonial Office 5/400. September 23rd, 1720. Letter to the Lords Justices
2. William P. Cummings. The South East in Early Maps. University of N. Carolina Press. 1958/1962. pp. 46-47,190 and Plate 48
3. Colonial Office 5/400. September 23, 1720. Letter to the Lords Justices
4. Journal of the Board of Trade, August 16, 1720

5. Colonial Office 323:7 K116
6. Historical Collections of S. Carolina, Vol. 1, p. 236

Chapter 2

1. Colonial Office 5/400, Sept. 23rd, 1720, op. cit., p.126
2. Ibid.
3. Colonial Office 5/358 A 19. A 21. A 23
4. Harold R. Shurtleff. The Log Cabin Myth. A Study of the Early Dwellings of the English Colonists in North America. repr. ed. (Gloucester: Peter Smith, 1967) p. 107
5. Richard J. Young. Blockhouses in Canada, 1749-1841: A Comparative Report and Catalogue. Canada Historic Sites, no. 23, 1969, p. 12
6. Op. cit. p. 56
7. British Public Record Office. Records relating to S. Carolina, Vol. 8, p. 170
8. Richard Arnold for the Secretary at War to Governor of Plymouth. War Office 4-23. 68. 4 October, 1720

Chapter 3

1. Historical Collections of S. Carolina, Vol. 1, p. 257
2. Ibid.
3. Ibid.
4. British Public Record Office. S. Carolina. British Journal, Vol. 1 d. 11/ Vol. 8, pp.179-181
5. Historical Collections of S. Carolina. Vol. 1, p. 257. Colonial Office 5/358 A. 34 (Letters & papers relating to Landing His Majesty's Independent Company now in South Carolina & ca, and likewise concerning Coll. Barnwell's going to Altamaha River in order to build a Small Fort there (16 folios), esp. Barnwell's memorial, June 3, 1721)

6. Colonial Office Records. 5/425. Legislative Journals, May, 1721 - February, 1723
7. Op. cit.
8. British Public Records Office. Vol. 9. pp.50-60
9. Ibid.
10. Five Carolina pounds represented one pound sterling in 18th century currency

Chapter 4

1. Col. Barnwell's Journal. Garrison at Alatamaha point. July, 1721 onwards, relating to his proceedings; published in The S. Carolina Historical & Genealogical Magazine, Vol. XXVII, No. 4, Oct. 1926, p. 193
2. Ibid. p. 195
3. "A Map or Plan of the Mouth of Alatamahaw with the adjacent Lands". c. 1721. Public Record Office, London. Colonial Office, Georgia, listed in Pre-Nineteenth Century Maps in the Collection of the Georgia Surveyor General Department, compiled by Janice Gayle Blake. 1975
4. Col. Barnwell's Journal. Garrison at Alatamaha point. July, 1721 onwards, relating to his proceedings; published in The S. Carolina Historical & Genealogical Magazine, Vol. XXVII, No. 4, Oct. 1926; July 13, 1721, p. 196
5. Op. cit. July 17, 1721, p. 197-8
6. Op. cit. July 21, 1721, p. 199
7. Op. cit. July 21, 1721, p. 200
8. Op. cit. July 29, 1721, p. 202
9. British Public Record Office, Vol. 9, Rec'd April 17, 1722 by Charles Hart, Sec.
10. Colonial Office 5/425. Legislative Journals for S. Carolina. May, 1721 - Feb., 1723. 13 August, 1721

11. Op. cit. Message to Governor & Council from Lower House, 26 August, 1721
12. "A Chart of St. Simons Harbour. September 2d, 1721", prepared by John Barnwell. Public Record Office, London. Colonial Office, Georgia 3, listed in Pre-Nineteenth Century Maps in the Collection of the Georgia Surveyor General Department, compiled by Janice Gayle Blake. 1975.
13. Colonial Office 5/425. Legislative Journals for S. Carolina. May, 1721 - Feb., 1723. Message to Governor & Council from Lower House, 16 September, 1721
14. Op. cit. Petition of John Barnwell, 16 September, 1721
15. Op. cit. Letter to Lower House from Governor, 16 September, 1721
16. Op. cit. Message from Governor to Assembly, 20 September, 1721

Chapter 5

1. The Story of an American Family. Stephen B. Barnwell. Marquette, 1969, p. 16
2. Colonial Office 5/425. Legislative Journals for S. Carolina. May, 1721 - Feb., 1723. Memorandum from Governor to Lower House, 19 February, 1722
3. Op. cit. Message from Lower House to Governor & Council, 15 February, 1722
4. Fulham Palace MSS. S. Carolina, no 117 (transcript, Library of Congress)
5. Colonial Office 5/425. Legislative Journals for S. Carolina. May, 1721 - Feb., 1723. Report of Committee of both Houses, 17 February, 1722, Item 16
6. Op. cit. Message from Governor. 19 February, 1722

Chapter 6

1. Colonial Office 5/425. Legislative Journals for S. Carolina. May, 1721 - Feb., 1723. Message from House to Governor. 28 February, 1722
2. Verner W. Crane. The Southern Frontier, 1670-1732. University of Michigan. 1929. p. 238
3. Ibid.
4. Colonial Office 5/358 A.103, A.104
5. Colonial Office 5/425. Legislative Journals for S. Carolina. May, 1721 - Feb., 1723. Message from Lower House to Governor, 8 March, 1722
6. Op. cit. Message from Governor, 9 March, 1722
7. Op. cit. Message to Governor, 24 May, 1722
8. Op. cit. Message to Governor, 14 June, 1722
9. Letter of 20 December, 1722, from Whitehall to King George I
10. British Public Record Office relating to S. Carolina, Vol. II, 1723-25, 9 February, 1723/4, p. 36
11. Colonial Office 5/425. Legislative Journals for S. Carolina. May, 1721 - Feb., 1723. Message to Assembly from Governor, 6 February, 1723

Chapter 7

1. Colonial Office 5/425. Legislative Journals for S. Carolina. May, 1721 - Feb., 1723. Message to Governor from Lower House, 20 March, 1722
2. Journal of Commons House of Assembly, 19 June, 1722. Commons House Journal, 1722-1724. Vol. VI, p. 31
3. Op. cit. Message to Lower House. 23 June, 1722
4. Council Journal, 24 November, 1722. Council Journal, 1722-1724, Vol. 2, p. 102
5. Op. cit. pp. 71-72

6. Colonial Office 5/425. Legislative Journals for S. Carolina. May, 1721 - Feb., 1723. Report of Committee of both Houses on Fort King George, 4 August, 1722

7. Op. cit. Deliberations of the House, 5 September, 1722

8. William P. Cummings, op. cit.

9. Colonial Office 5/425. Legislative Journals for S. Carolina. May, 1721 - Feb., 1723. Deliberations of the House, 5 September, 1722

10. Larry E. Ivers. British Drums on the Southern Frontier. Military Colonization of Georgia. 1733-1749. Chapel Hill, 1974. p. 25

11. Colonial Office 5/425. Legislative Journals for S. Carolina. May, 1721 - Feb., 1723. 5 September, 1722

12. Op. cit. 27 September, 1722

13. Council Journal, 1722-1724. Vol. 2, p. 111. Letter of 30 October, 1722, to Governor recorded on 5 December, 1722

14. Colonial Office 5/425. Legislative Journals for S. Carolina. May, 1721 - February, 1723. Letter from Governor, 6 February, 1723

15. Council Journal, June 9, 1724. Council Journal 1722-1724, Vol. 2, p. 264

16. British-American Officers, 1720-1763. Compiled by W. R. Williams. The S. Carolina Historical & Genealogical Magazine, Vol. XXXIII, no. 3, July, 1932

17. Copy of Will, Probate Court Records, Charleston Co., South Carolina

Chapter 8

1. Council Journal 1722-1724, Vol. 2, p. 278, 11 June, 1724

2. British Public Record Office, Vol. 10, p. 299/Historical Collections of S. Carolina, Vol. 1, p. 236/ Colonial Office 5/387. f. 73

3. Ibid.
4. British Public Record Office, Vol. 11, p. 7
5. Ibid.
6. Colonial Office 5/425. Legislative Journals of S. Carolina. May, 1721 - Feb., 1723. 14 February, 1722
7. Colonial Office 5/360 C 2 (enclosure)
8. Ibid.
9. Verner W. Crane. Op. cit. p. 247
10. Council Journal. Vol. 4, p. 171
11. British Public Record Office, Records relating to S. Carolina, Vol. 3/Colonial Office 5/360 C. 8

Chapter 9

1. Public Records of S. Carolina, Vol. 11, pp. 268-271. Enclosure to letter to Duke of Newcastle/Colonial Office 5/383, no. 30 ii
2. Public Records of S. Carolina, Vol. 14, pp. 204-205
3. British Public Record Office, Vol. 3, C/25 & Vol. 13, p. 58
4. Larry E. Ivers, op. cit. p. 10
5. Council Journal, S. Carolina, 1730-1734, Vol V, p. 451
6. Colonial Office 5/400, pp. 283-376
7. Colonial Office 5/362 D 1
8. Council Record, S. Carolina, Vol. V, p. 170, 26 February, 1731
9. Public Records of S. Carolina, Vol. 16, p. 73
10. Larry E. Ivers, op. cit, p. 50
11. Bessie Lewis. The Story of Old Fort King George. The first English settlement in the land which is now Georgia. October, 1932

BIBLIOGRAPHY

OFFICIAL RECORDS

London, England :
Colonial Office Records
Journals of the Board of Trade
War Office Records
South Carolina/British Journals
British Public Record Office Records relating to South Carolina
Colonial Office - Legislative Journals for South Carolina

Columbia, South Carolina -
Department of Archives & History :
Historical Collections of South Carolina
Council Journals
Fulham Palace MSS. South Carolina (transcript, Library of Congress)
Journal of Commons House of Assembly
Public Records of South Carolina

Charleston County, South Carolina :
Probate Court Records

Atlanta, Georgia -
Georgia Department of Archives & History :
St. Andrew's Parish Plat Books
Pre-Nineteenth Century Map Collection

Athens, Georgia - Hargrett Rare Book and Manuscript Library, University of Georgia Libraries :
Eighteenth century maps of Southeast United States

Savannah, Georgia -
Georgia Historical Society :
British Public Record Office Records relating to Georgia (copies)
Margaret Davis Cate Collection

McIntosh County, Darien, Georgia -
County Courthouse :
Title Deeds

BOOKS, ARTICLES AND PAMPHLETS

BARNWELL, Colonel John. Journal of Colonel John Barnwell (Tuscarora) in the Construction of the Fort on the Altamaha in 1721, in "Barnwell, Joseph W. Fort King George". The South Carolina Historical & Genealogical Magazine, Vol. XXVII, no. 4, Oct., 1926

BARNWELL, Stephen B. The Story of An American Family. Marquette. 1969

BARTRAM, William. Travels in Georgia and Florida, 1773-74. A Report to Dr. John Fothergill. Vol. 1 (Georgia), annotated by Francis Harper in Transactions of the American Philosophical Society, n.s. Vol. 3, part 2. American Philosophical Society, Philadelphia. 1943

BLAKE, Janice Gayle. Compilation of Pre-Nineteenth Century Maps in the Collection of the Georgia Surveyor General Department. Atlanta, State Printing Office, 1975

CRANE, Verner W. The Southern Frontier, 1670-1732. University of Michigan Press. 1929. 3rd printing, 1964

CUMMINGS, William P. The South East in Early Maps. University of North Carolina Press. 1958/1962

IVERS, Larry E. British Drums on the Southern Frontier. Military Colonization of Georgia. 1733-1749. Chapel Hill, 1974

KELSO, William M. Excavations at the Fort King George Historical Site, Darien, Georgia. The 1967 Survey. Georgia Historical Commission. Archaeological Research Series. Number One, 1968

KING, Reuben. Journal, 1800-1806. Collections of the Georgia Historical Society. Vol. XV. Edited by Virginia Steele Wood & Ralph van Wood. 1971

LEWIS, Bessie. Old Fort King George : The First English Settlement in the Land which is now Georgia. Privately printed, Oct., 1932

SHURTLEFF, Harold R. The Log Cabin Myth. A Study of the Early Dwellings of the English Colonists in North America. repr. ed. (Gloucester : Peter Smith, 1967)

WILLIAMS, W.R. British-American Officers, 1720-1763. The South Carolina Historical & Genealogical Magazine, Vol. XXXIII, no. 3, July, 1932

YOUNG, Richard J. Blockhouses in Canada, 1749-1841 : A Comparative Report & Catalogue. Canada Historic Sites. No. 23, 1969

JEANNINE COOK, artist and writer, became immersed in Fort King George's history when her husband, Rundle, undertook to raise the funds necessary for the Fort's reconstruction in McIntosh County, coastal Georgia. A 'citizen of the world' since leaving her native Tanzania, she has written for such publications as Smithsonian and Connoisseur magazines. Her drawings and watercolours have won numerous awards in exhibitions throughout the United States.